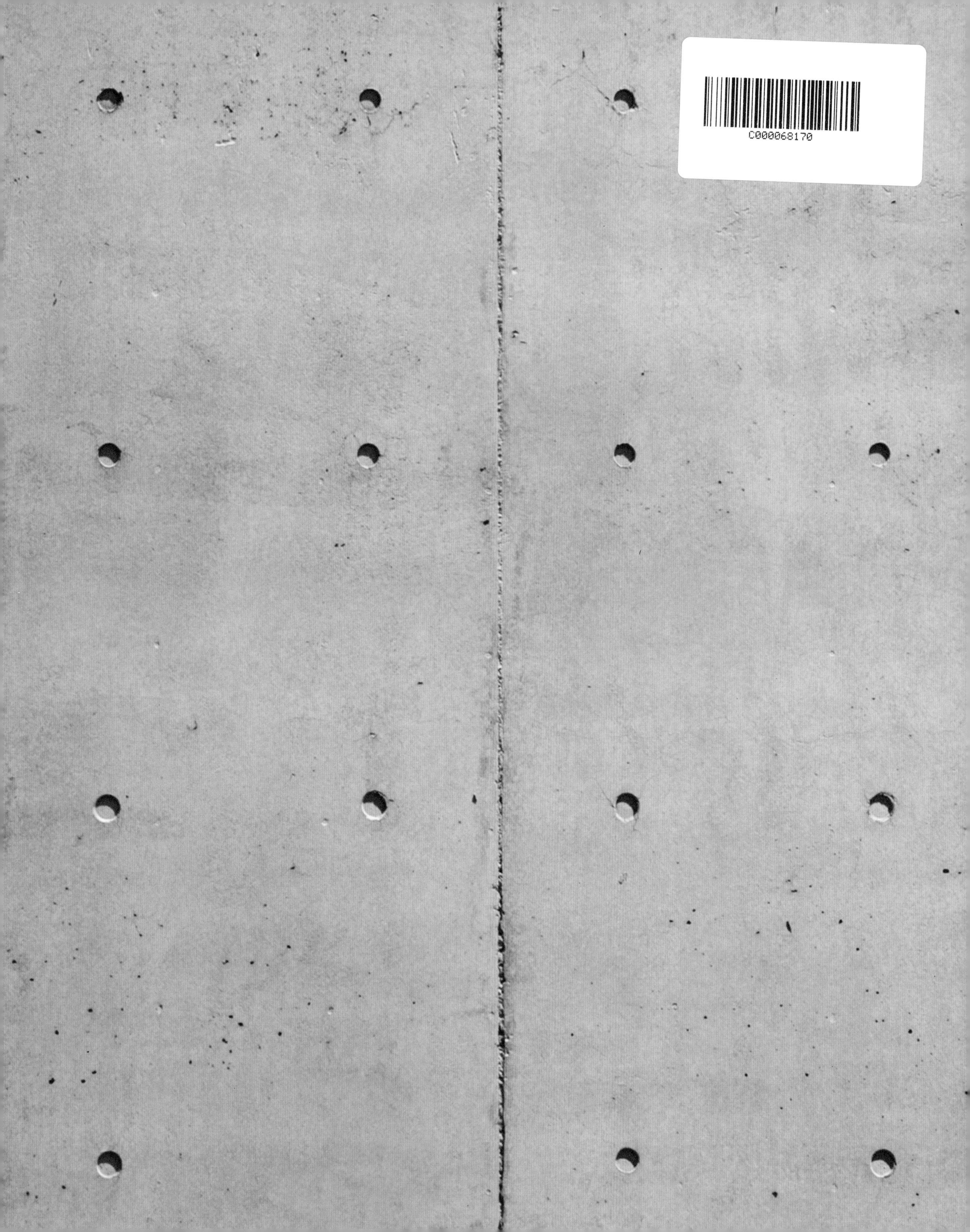

ASSASSIN'S CREED

INTO THE ANIMUS

ASSASSIN'S CREED

INTO THE ANIMUS

INSIDE A FILM CENTURIES IN THE MAKING

IAN NATHAN

FOREWORD BY GÉRARD GUILLEMOT

TITAN BOOKS

An Insight Editions Book

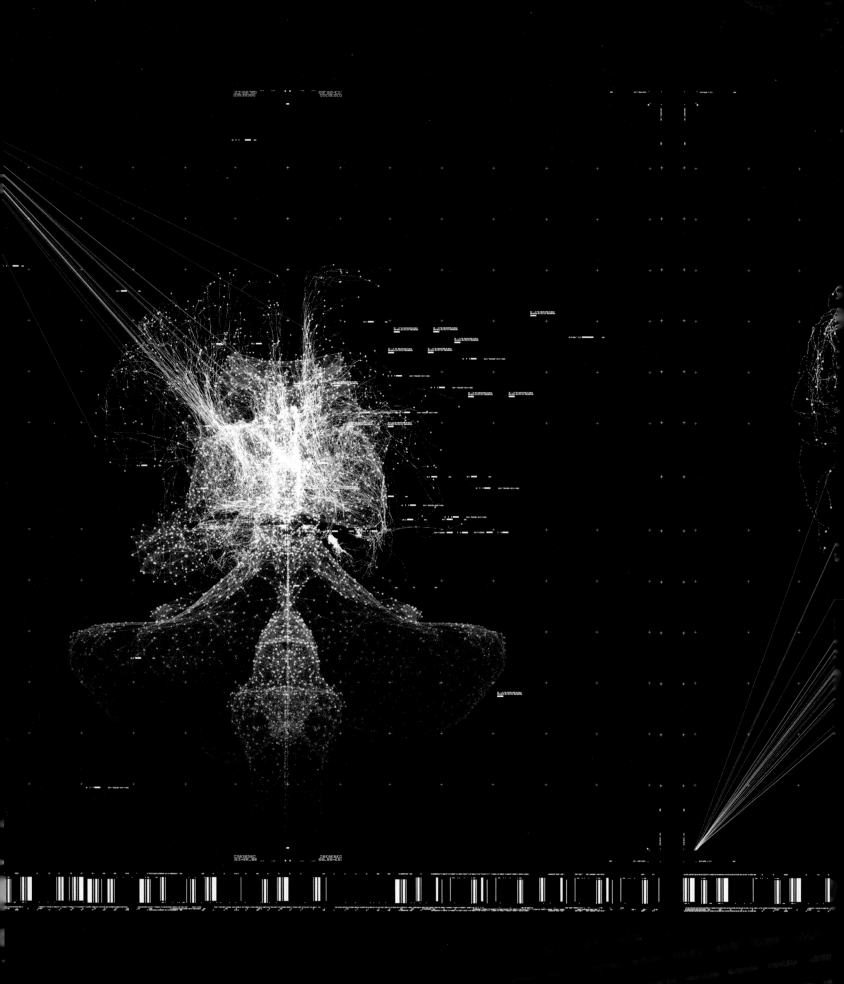

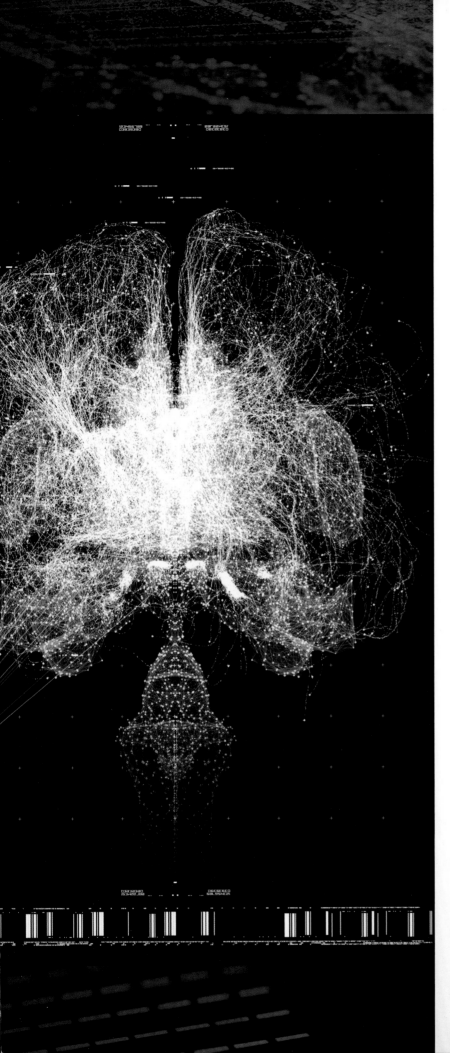

CONTENTS

FOREWORD

MAKING THE *ASSASSIN'S CREED* MOVIE has been an adventure. Until now, games have been adapted into movies independent of the game creators, and the filmmakers have not necessarily understood the gist of the game. So we knew that Ubisoft had to find the right partners to work with on our first film. But we had to be patient.

For five years, there were discussions with many actors and directors, but it was only when we met Michael Fassbender, our star and producer—and then director Justin Kurzel—that we were confident we could create something special.

In the past, game adaptations have been seen only as action movies, and producers thought that they just needed a director who was good with action films. So the stunts and special effects might be great, but the film would lack a human dimension. When Justin was brought on as director, I loved that he had already taken risks. When you do a Shakespearean adaptation, as he did with *Macbeth*, you are taking a risk. You accept that pressure. And it shows that you are able to take other mediums, like theater or games, into account and create a new entity that still reflects those origins.

Justin was not afraid to go for something that is really groundbreaking, to find a new way to express what is in the game. For example, the Animus—the device through which the hero experiences the past—was simply a chair in the game. In the film, Justin created this huge mechanical arm that is attached to the main character, Callum, and moves him through the air. Then images of his Assassin ancestor, Aguilar, are superimposed into the Animus chamber with stunning visual effects. These are not synthetic images but layers of real images. I have never seen anything like it before. Honestly, Justin has made a film that is so much more than pure action. He has been able to express the human meaning of the whole Assassin's Creed concept.

Michael Fassbender's level of commitment has been extraordinary. This is a very important project for him, and he has been a great believer. He played a vital role in the story development. He worked with the game developers in order to understand the intention behind each element and how it could be translated into a story. And he is such a special actor. He likes to move between different contexts, different stories, and he does it so well. With some actors, you know the minute you see them that they will win the day. Michael keeps everybody on their toes until the end. Even the other Assassins think he's dangerous.

We always knew that the concept of Assassin's Creed went far beyond a great series of games. It really is a very human story. It is about how the past impacts who we are. It is about the concept of free will and control. It is about seeing things as more than just black and white: the Templars are the bad guys, the Assassins the good guys. But the Templars want a functioning society to keep people safe and organized; the Assassins want to enforce the opposite. These are big themes.

And there is also spectacle. The film has enormous battles and shows all the moves of the game in the real world: jumping from one building to another, running sideways along walls, and leaping from crazy heights.

Ubisoft has reached a place where every time it brings out a new game, people know that it has been made with great care and attention to quality. With this first Ubisoft movie, we can say the same. It is not just an adaptation; it is something we can be proud of, something beyond pure entertainment. I think people will be talking about this movie for years to come.

Our patience has really paid off.

Gérard Guillemot
CEO Ubisoft Motion Pictures

PREVIOUS PAGES: Animus graphics showing a brain desynchronized with the machine.

RIGHT: Aguilar's initiation into the Assassin Brotherhood.

CHAPTER 1

RISE OF THE ASSASSIN

THE PERFECT ASSASSIN

IT WAS OVER FIVE YEARS AGO that the Ubisoft Motion Pictures team met with Ubisoft's CEO Yves Guillemot to discuss the potential of Assassin's Creed for big-screen treatment. It was essential, Guillemot insisted, that the DNA of the games be respected in any attempt to translate them to another medium. Ubisoft was eager to build upon the backbone of its great successes—Prince of Persia, Splinter Cell, and Assassin's Creed—to expand from a game company to an entertainment company and set up their own movie studio. The worlds they created had great potential beyond the realm of video games. And that meant finding the right actor to play the lead Assassin in a film.

They met the perfect Assassin in a London restaurant. It was nothing fancy, just a regular sort of place. A place that wouldn't draw too much attention. A game changing meeting between Ubisoft Motion Pictures (UMP) and future producer and star Michael Fassbender. "The perfect Assassin," Jean de Rivieres, Executive Producer, says of Fassbender, looking back on this significant moment in the development of the epic video game franchise into a feature film. An adaptation Ubisoft Motion Pictures was determined would redefine the idea of video games on the big screen.

From the start, the intention was to fashion something truly exceptional from the franchise created by Ubisoft that has so far spawned ten core games, as well as novels and comic books—a great action film but with the character-driven depth that is a hallmark of the Assassin's Creed games. Producer Jean-Julien Baronnet called it a "high-content movie." They wanted to make a mainstream movie with big ideas and moral complexity.

Rather than creating a list of stars, the UMP team had instead written a list of characteristics and qualities that made for the perfect Assassin. Almost instinctively, they decided upon Michael Fassbender for the lead role.

With experience in both period pieces as well as physically demanding action roles, Fassbender was a like-minded individual. One glance at his filmography easily demonstrates how he mixed lauded indies (*Hunger*, *Shame*, and *12 Years a Slave*) with more mainstream films—but no less fuelled with exotic ideas—like *X-Men: First Class* or *Prometheus*. He embodied exactly what they were trying to achieve, physically and psychologically.

So in late 2011, de Rivieres, along with Baronnet, met in a quiet corner of London, talking the German-Irish actor through the extraordinary world behind the game: how a secret war between the Assassins and the Templars has raged throughout history. And how a contemporary hero, using the technology known as the Animus, taps into memories buried within his DNA and sees through the eyes of his ancestor. This ancestor, they explained, would prove to be one of the greatest heroes of the Assassin's Brotherhood.

They didn't have a script or a studio yet; they just talked, and Fassbender began to ask questions. Within ten minutes he was telling them how much he loved the idea. "The first thing that jumped out at me was this concept of DNA memory," Fassbender recalls, enticed by the feasibility

ABOVE: Michael Fassbender filming an up-close assassination on location in Almeria.

OPPOSITE BOTTOM: Callum's execution is only the beginning.

of the idea. "When you've got something scientifically based, it elevates a fantasy story so much more, because an audience can believe it."

DNA memory gave a solid foundation to the conflict and drama between these two camps, the Templars and Assassins, battling since the birth of mankind. And Fassbender was excited by how their eternal dust-up came with "lots of gray areas." How could the Assassins be the good guys if they kill, even in pursuit of a higher purpose? Why are the Templars the villains if they hope to help mankind? He could see, immediately, that this was epic and thrilling material, but far from conventional.

Three hours later, de Rivieres and Baronnet shook Fassbender's hand and invited him to Paris to meet members of the game development team and immerse himself in the universe. A week later, he was signed on for the project. But even back on that first afternoon, the UMP team knew they had their Assassin. All they needed now was a script, a director, and a studio.

ORIGIN OF A BRAND

IN THE EARLY 2000s, Ubisoft was developing a follow-up to *Prince of Persia: The Sands of Time*, the latest game in the successful fantasy series. They began to develop a more realistic setting for the sequel, building a new Assassin character with that realism in mind. A definite shift from the *Prince of Persia*'s Arabian Nights–style fantasia, they found they were developing an entirely new intellectual property ("IP"). By 2006, Ubisoft had established the idea of a modern character—a cypher for the player—who uses genetic memory to experience the life of his ancestor, a medieval Assassin who could climb, swing, and leap across rooftops using an animated version of the French street-running sport known as parkour. Set in a historically meticulous Middle East at the time of the Third Crusade, *Assassin's Creed* was released to great acclaim in 2007.

Speaking with the kind of in-depth appreciation and unbridled enthusiasm that comes from years of immersion in the franchise, Aymar Azaïzia, Assassin's Creed's Brand Content Director, believes it was the concept of fighting for a cause and meting out justice that struck a chord with fans. "You become a part of intense historical moments in the game," he says. "Assassin's Creed gives the fans a chance to meet historical characters and become a major player in many of the conflicts and battles throughout history." The premise was empowering, allowing the player to have a say in the minute workings of history.

TOP LEFT: Early concept art by Khai Nguyen for the *Assassin's Creed* game.

TOP RIGHT: Artwork of Aguilar escaping from Spanish soldiers by performing the Leap of Faith off a bridge.

While the action was intimate, the setting was vast. This was the birth of the open world game. "You have a lot of options on what do to and where to go," Azaïzia explains. "You're in control of your agenda. It empowers the player." Moreover, rather than a creating a fantasy realm, Ubisoft offered hyper-detailed historical tourism. History, Azaïzia likes to say, is part of the franchise's DNA. Hence the motto: "History is our playground."

Over subsequent sequels, and utilizing the advancing in-game technology of the Animus, Ubisoft would visit new time periods and new characters. In the various iterations, the series has traveled to Renaissance Italy, the American Revolution, the pirate-haunted waters of the Caribbean, the French Revolution, Imperial China, Victorian-era London on the cusp of the Industrial Revolution, the Sikh Empire in India, the October Revolution that swept Russia into chaos, among others.

Each setting represented a pivotal moment of upheaval and change, but also of revolutions in art, science, and philosophy; mankind at its very worst and best. Together they presented a giant tapestry of history upon which fact and fiction were woven. Gamers could meet historical figures as diverse as Leonardo Da Vinci and Charles Darwin, and freerun across locations such as the dizzying heights of the Notre Dame Cathedral or the bedlam of London's Piccadilly Circus circa 1868. Against each background the eternal battle between Assassins and Templars would be reconvened. Death-defying action combined with intellectual ideas, what could be more cinematic?

Assassin's Creed presented great opportunities for storytelling. This would be an expansion of the universe, not an adaptation of any particular game. The burning questions were what the movie would be about and when was it going to be set. All of recorded time was open to them; this universe is literally boundless. Nevertheless, bearing in mind what was fundamental to the game, they needed turmoil, a pivotal moment in history. The location and time period had to both be somewhere fresh to gamers and offer the familiar architecture across which the Assassin could climb and leap, defying gravity. It didn't take long before they hit upon the Inquisition in fifteenth-century Spain, locating their story in Seville and Granada where the last of the Moorish forces held out. Catholicism was clashing with Islam in cityscapes forested in towers, ledges, bridges, and parapets as far as the eyes can see. Not to mention the high probability of plunging to your death in the streets below.

BELOW: The Muslim Emir Muhammed XVII, Tomás de Torquemada of the Inquisition, and the Templar soldier Ojeda inside the Court of Lions.

OPPOSITE: Maria and Aguilar face the wrath of the Inquisition.

"There were also stories we could play with," de Rivieres explains; "potential cameos and ideas that could link with it." This was the time of the dreaded Torquemada, as well as intrepid explorer Christopher Columbus.

Once it was out there, there was no putting it back in the box. They had their historical playground.

We are still feeling the reverberations of the era today. The Inquisition had an enormous effect in the creation of the Spanish nation, and Granada's fall was very important historically as well. In 1491, King Ferdinand II and Queen Isabella I were using the Inquisition to unify Spain under one religion—the Catholic Church—squeezing the barons for gold to fund their wars, otherwise they'd end up roasting in Hell, if not somewhere more local. There was one city that held out— Granada, resplendent on the Southern coast. Governed by the Muslim Emir Muhammad XII, Jews, Christians, Muslims, and Moors lived in relative harmony. Thus Granada was a threat not only to the credibility of the Inquisition and its ruthless figurehead, Tomás de Torquemada, but the very idea of a universal Catholic God. Hence all of the Inquisition's might was bent on overthrowing Muhammad, and the fall of Granada in 1492 led to the birth of the Spanish nation.

Into this furnace come the Assassins and the Templars, each with their own agendas.

FORGING A MOVIE

WHILE THE DEVELOPMENT TEAM toiled away in fifteenth-century Spain, Fassbender made six movies, in worlds as diverse as *Macbeth* and *X-Men: Apocalypse*, but if anything, he became more involved with *Assassin's Creed*. Via regular conference calls and occasional meetings, he helped to develop not only his character but also the entire fabric of the movie. "When we first sat down I had just set up a production company, DMC Film," Fassbender says, "and I wanted to be part of it as producer. To help develop the story right from the beginning."

From a plot perspective, the script was a challenge. Normally a film centers around one hero and one antagonist. The plot is attached to the hero and follows his or her arc. And usually it stays in one time period.

With *Assassin's Creed*, they were confronted with *two* heroes: one in the present, Callum, and the other, Aguilar, in the past. There are two villains, past and present. And they are all intimately connected. Furthermore, the modern day characters do not actually travel to the past; they observe it from the present. So the Inquisition sequences, in a sense, exist within the same timeline as the Abstergo sequences like a parallel universe.

The first challenge was to make the two heroes of the same lineage—and played by the same actor—while recognizing that they are different characters. "We all agreed that the present day character should carry the story," de Rivieres says. "The story follows Callum's character arc. The difficulty was making sure the past nourishes the story of the present."

They devised a dynamic where the Templars—under the guise of a present day corporation called Abstergo Industries—hook up Callum into the Animus and make him relive the memories of his ancestor Aguilar, a newly initiated Assassin, who haunts the conflicts of Southern Spain outside of the jurisdiction of the Inquisition. Abstergo is certain, as Callum helplessly witnesses events from the Animus, that Aguilar will lead them to where a powerful artifact has been secreted.

The second challenge was how to bridge the two storylines. How would each feed the other? Their answer lay in the Animus itself. Not only did the technology offer a unique cinematic vision, it also solved many of their narrative issues. By bridging the two characters through the Animus, Callum's ancestor could help him to learn about his own life.

In other words, experiencing Aguilar's memories transforms Callum from death row inmate to Assassin. He would absorb the experience of being Aguilar in an entirely cinematic way: Step-by-step, we *see* how Aguilar "teaches" Callum to the point where Callum realizes that he hasn't decided to become an Assassin, he was *born one*. They now had their hero's journey, and the themes they wanted to explore. For instance, the cost of free will.

The Templars believe that eradicating violence could mean an end to war. The question is, at what cost? Violence could be an inevitable side effect of free will, and the Assassins think that free will is essential to human nature. Would we still be human beings without it? The movie places the audience in the middle of that debate.

Indeed, the entire ethos of Assassin's Creed is founded on a contradiction—the members of this secret society dedicated to peace and freedom are killers by trade. They are individualists bound by a tradition.

PREVIOUS PAGES: Michael Fassbender and Jeremy Irons on set in London; Michael Fassbender and a stunt double as Callum and Aguilar.

OPPOSITE: Often a silent figure, Aguilar's actions speak volumes as to his character and ideals.

ABOVE: The graffiti and sketches in Callum's cell contain hidden iconography, including a Templar cross on the wall to the right.

Ubisoft was determined to maintain their freedom within the studio system. While they needed a studio to help bring their film to fruition, and market and distribute it worldwide, they wanted to maintain creative control. They presented a package with the script, the budget, the director, and the lead actors to New Regency (whose diverse output includes *Fight Club*, *The Revenant*, and *12 Years a Slave*).

Assassin's Creed was already a coveted project in Hollywood, and Ubisoft wasn't short of suitors. In October 2012 they announced that their film would be a co-production with New Regency with distribution by 20th Century Fox. With Fassbender playing not one but two contrasting protagonists, the script's intricate structure, and a renowned production studio, the creation of the film was set to be a journey of epic proportions.

GAMES AND FILMS

A PLAYER CAN SPEND between 60 to 100 hours completing an Assassin's Creed game. With only two to three hours to tell a story, a film and a game are very different experiences. In the game, the player is the actor in an interactive story, rather than solely the audience.

Nevertheless, it was important that their film not be entirely divorced from the experience of the game and the fans it had built up over the years. They had to recognize that they were still part of that tradition. There were certain "red line rules" that couldn't be broken. For instance, the past could not be altered—Callum can only observe Aguilar's actions from within; he cannot redirect them. All the complexities of time travel in science fiction cinema do not apply to *Assassin's Creed*. People live and die as history dictates.

BELOW: Concept art of a ravaged Granada in the wake of the Inquisition's attack.

Indeed, above all, both film and game would share the same dedication to making the historical period as accurate as possible down to the fabric used for the costumes, the mosaics on a church floor, and the intricate geography of the city streets.

Caroline Sol, Ubisoft's Head of Creative Content Services, was responsible for upholding the games' and now the film's historical and scientific veracity. She launched herself into researching not only the fixtures and fittings of the Inquisition, but scientific threads like DNA memory. "I really had to find out information on things that do not yet exist," she says.

If history and science were to be treated with the utmost respect, so must the tenets of the game. Sol was also responsible for putting together bibles of information on the game for the director and each of his heads of department.

"I had to collect together everything we had on the Assassin's Creed universe," Sol said. This involved rooting out concept art going back years. "I had four hundred inspirational pages of images: costumes, props, weapons . . ."

So, as much as game and film differ, they also share a lot of the same elements. The film's plot, introducing the Assassins and the Templars, discovering their conflicting motives, the quest to find or protect the artifact, and the tension over whether the modern-day hero might be seduced by the Templars, involves many of the same points as the first iteration of the game *Assassin's Creed*.

Azaïzia explains how important it is not to overwhelm the newcomer to this world. "You're dropped into a universe. You don't know the rules. You don't know what's happening. And you're going to see the events through the eyes of your main hero."

ABOVE: Maria evades capture inside a nobleman's house.

OPPOSITE: Early concept of the Apple of Eden.

Even so, as we will come to see, the film was also filled with Easter Eggs, references, and visual motifs for the ardent Assassin's Creed fans. There are secrets hidden in the walls of certain scenes that will take hours of freeze-framing on blu-ray to decipher.

When it came to the Assassins' abilities, the producers wanted to echo the character animation in the game. Fans can spot signature moves. Special attention was paid to the Leap of Faith, the graceful dive from a terrifying height that has become the iconic franchise image.

"We treated the fans like heroes," de Rivieres says. There was an on-going dialogue via social media, a testing of the waters on their new ideas. Also, via Azaïzia, there was continuous brain-storming with the game-makers at Ubisoft. As de Rivieres says: "There was a link between brand and the movie all the way through."

Very subtly, the film embraced the arcane mythology of the game universe, which proposes the existence of an ancient alien race that created humankind in their image. While never mentioned directly, their handiwork is most definitely present in the film. The "First Civilization" boasted fantastically complex technology, and a number of their powerful artifacts remain on Earth, known as the Pieces of Eden. The Templars are hell-bent on getting their hands on all the artifacts, because each possesses a powerful scientific and technological property.

THE PERFECT DIRECTOR

ALTHOUGH THERE WAS A LOT OF INTEREST by many directors, the producers felt strongly about going with an independent director who would bring something personal to the film. Fassbender suggested Justin Kurzel.

Fassbender was filming *Macbeth* under Justin's direction in Scotland's windblown Isle of Skye and England's bleak Northumbria when he recommended the director for *Assassin's Creed*.

"There is a very visceral sense to the way he made his films that I just thought would work really well with the game," Fassbender explains. *Macbeth* had been a great experience, and he and Kurzel had recognized kindred spirits in one another. Fassbender could see that he was a director who pursued a truth within the material, unwilling, almost unable to compromise.

Born in Gawler, South Australia, Kurzel is a former theatrical set designer who began his directing career with the formidable *Snowtown*, loosely based on real-life serial killer John Bunting who preyed upon those he saw as sexual deviants in the Adelaide suburbs. Having grown up close to the gruesome murders, it was a story Kurzel knew well, and his overwhelming version of events garnered passionate reviews and became a cult hit. Fassbender loved it and approached the director about *Macbeth*. Undaunted about working with stars of the calibre of Fassbender and Marion Cotillard, who would play the roll of Lady Macbeth, Kurzel could see the potential in revisiting Shakespeare.

Both of Kurzel's films are invested with an extraordinary visual power. *Macbeth*, especially, feasts on the authentic re-creation of Scotland in 1057—a violent world of rival fiefdoms, where religion jostles for supremacy with the supernatural.

THESE PAGES: Justin Kurzel with Michael Fassbender and Marion Cotillard.

It wasn't long before UMP met with Kurzel to discuss the film. The director shared his vision quickly and clearly. He gave them detailed notes on the script. And they really liked what he had to say. The film team realized very quickly that they wanted Kurzel as director for his independent style and values.

"We loved what we saw, we loved what we heard, and we loved the passion and style and eloquence in how he spoke," de Rivieres says. "He's character-oriented."

Nonetheless, untested on a film of this scale, Kurzel was another leap of faith.

The director can remember the exact moment Fassbender sat him down and told him about the project. "I was literally halfway through the edit of *Macbeth*," he recalls, "and Michael said, 'There's this film, and it is about someone who discovers who they are through the memory of his ancestors.' And I thought that was really intriguing. And he said, 'It's inspired by Assassin's Creed.'"

Kurzel admits he didn't have much experience with gaming beyond trying to get the high score on *Double Dragon* in a local mall as a teenager. However, visiting Ubisoft headquarters in Paris and discovering the effort and passion that went into each game, and the entire culture that surrounded Assassin's Creed was a real eye opener. "There was a narrative and a vision," he says. "It had a purpose beyond just entertainment."

The budget was far greater than anything he had worked with, but as a sure sign of his determination to bring his own signature to the material, he pushed hard to use his *Macbeth* cinematographer Adam Arkapaw.

Fassbender agreed. "It was important that Adam came with him, because they have such a shorthand. That put us in a good place. We really wanted to highlight the look of the two worlds, the starkness of the present and the richness of the regression."

Once Kurzel and Arkapaw were signed up, they began to rework the script yet again, investing it with the director's vision.

"It needed a central journey in terms of who the lead protagonist was," Kurzel says. "The challenge of Assassin's Creed is that the concept is really complex—the idea of a modern day character who goes into this machine called the Animus and that takes him back in time. But it's not a time travel machine; it's a memory travel machine. You have two different time periods, and one actor that is playing two different characters."

The key was creating a strong central storyline in terms of who the lead character was and resolving that story by the end of the film. Kurzel realized that this was in effect an origin story.

"It's about a man who discovers who he is through the experiences of those who have come before him," he explains. "That is an integral and dynamic part of the concept of Assassin's Creed that I think elevates it from just being a game. It is actually a fantastic starting point to write a film."

ABOVE: On set in Hunstville State Prison.

OPPOSITE: Stunt master Ben Cooke demonstrates the technique for Maria's drop off the roof.

Soon after came the key addition of production designer Andy Nicholson. Veteran of projects as diverse as *Sleepy Hollow* and *Gravity*, Nicholson brings a scientific exactitude to his films. He uses 3D modeling techniques, aiming to extract a working reality from every world he creates, no matter how bizarre (*Charlie and the Chocolate Factory*) or far-flung (*Troy*). He was thrilled by the duality *Assassin's Creed* offered: the futuristic palate of Abstergo and the flamboyant historical detail of Inquisition-era Spain.

"One of the nice things about this film was that Ubisoft was open to us exploring ideas for how to change the medium from a game to a movie," he says. "There are fundamental things in terms of how the game operates that we had to refine, play around with, riff on, to make a better movie."

Both Kurzel and Nicholson were of one accord that the film would resist, at all costs, the temptation to depend on computer-generated imagery (CGI) to create their world. They used special effects to enhance, not replace.

In other words, if a scene were humanly possible, they would do it for real.

For Kurzel, it was simply a question of how to make the gameplay feel like a cinematic experience. What happens if you do a real Leap of Faith? What if you actually saw Assassins jump from building to building?

"The great thing about cinema," he says, "is that you can bring that human element into it, where the audience responds to watching real human beings actually put the effort and danger into doing those things. So it was about celebrating what is humanly possible. I never wanted the film to feel like a superhero movie. I wanted you to look at it and think, 'Wow there are human beings doing that, and they are doing it like Olympians.'"

There were, of course, limits to practical effects. Fifteenth-century Granada and Seville have long since been consigned to history. In terms of extended backgrounds and specific detailing, computers would create the bustling sprawl of old Spain. Some scenes were too risky for the cast and stunt men, and they would need to remove the paraphernalia of filmmaking such as wires and cranes. The Animus, in all its exotic detail, was very much predicated on computer effects.

And yet, stunt master Ben Cooke estimates the film to be 80 percent practical and 20 percent digital.

"There's a danger to films that are creatively inside a kind of box, filmed on a parking lot with green screen," Kurzel says. "You can feel their artifice. For *Assassin's Creed*, having that sense of danger about it, that sense of realism, breathes oxygen into the film."

With a director at the helm, and with this being their first feature film, the team at Ubisoft Motion Pictures agreed that it would benefit all of them to bring on a fellow producer with experience at this level of filmmaking. Frank Marshall has been involved in some of the most successful and beloved films ever made: *Raiders of the Lost Ark, Back to the Future,* the *Bourne* trilogy, and most recently, *Jurassic World*. He was a figurehead of the kind of thoughtful blockbuster they were striving to echo.

"He was perfectly complementary to who we were," de Rivieres says. "He gave so much to the project. He went to the UK for the entire shoot. He was the wise force in the room."

Without any experience with the video game, Marshall is content to think of himself as representing the general movie-going audience. "It's important to have the two worlds merge," he says, meaning fan and non-fan. "It's a complicated, interesting story. You've got to set up the rules of the game. How you do that is the trick."

Marshall defines his role as dealing with all the logistics of preparation, budget, location, and being the go-between with the studio, so that Kurzel and his team could get on with making their film. According to Marshall, it was his job "to keep the movie going." Scheduling, weather, and the logistics of moving this huge production around Malta and Spain all came down to Marshall's planning. "I had to look at the show from high above with a big, wide-angle lens," he says. While on location they would often have only a day or two in a busy marketplace or on a church roof, and it was Marshall who had to make sure they still had the space to capture the scene.

ASSEMBLING THE CAST

WITH KURZEL AND HIS INNER TEAM in place, they began to fill out the cast. They were thrilled to cast Fassbender's *Macbeth* companion Marion Cotillard as Sofia, the chief scientist at Abstergo and one of the most morally complex characters in the film. "I heard about the movie before they proposed me taking a role in it," says the French star whose work has varied between her Oscar-winning performance in *La Vie en Rose* and the likes of *The Dark Knight Rises* and *Inception*. "They held writing sessions in Southwest France just near my house. So I knew that they were writing this movie, and later they asked me to be part of it."

She had never played the game (or any game), but was really impressed by the script. "It was really a reflection on the origin of violence. Also I loved with working with Justin and Michael and to be reunited for a very different project was very exciting."

For Rikkin, head of the Templars and ostensibly the villain of the piece, they called upon eloquent, sinewy British actor Jeremy Irons. After an extensive search, French actress Ariane Labed was chosen for the part of Maria, a fellow Assassin close to Aguilar. Brendan Gleeson would play Joseph, Callum's father, a shadow of a man after repeated sessions in the Animus.

"As with all my casts, it was just actors that I loved," Kurzel says of his casting philosophy. It was very much about finding the people who best fit the characters. "A lot of it was just instinct," he admits. "Who I thought was great and wanted to work with."

With the team assembled, production commenced on *Assassin's Creed* on August 27, 2015—an epic shoot that would go through the first weeks of 2016.

OPPOSITE: An iconic Maria pose.

TOP: Marion Cotillard filming a scene in London.

ABOVE: Callum's choices throughout the film redefine both his past and future.

CHAPTER 2

ABSTERGO

INTRODUCING CALLUM

CALLUM'S STORY BEGINS IN THE PAST, with an eagle's cry and a view of the desert from above. Except this is not Spain of 1491, but New Mexico in 1988.

The New Mexico prelude, filmed for efficiency in Almeria on the coast of Spain, sets into motion vital plot and character developments that will evolve as the film progresses. The twelve-year old Callum (Angus Brown) returns home to find that his father has murdered his mother.

Cut to: death row, present day. The adult Callum has killed a man and is awaiting his execution. Callum saw something that no child should see, and it has filled him with rage as an adult—an almost unbearable sense of injustice. He is driven by violence. He doesn't trust anyone.

Fassbender says, "Callum's very much dislocated from society and doesn't belong to any family as such. They were taken away from him. He's been institutionalised one way or the other his whole life. Be it at a young offender's institute or a prison." Spiritually he is an empty vessel.

As Justin Kurzel sees it, Callum has grown up having this violence in him but no idea where it comes from. In a sense, as Callum says in the film, it protects him. The only thing that gets him through is being able to defend himself. "I found that really interesting," says the director. "It is not until he is aware that he is part of the Creed, and that Creed is actually quite violent, that he is truly able to focus those instincts towards a particular kind of order."

The contrast between Callum and Aguilar, his Assassin forebear, is pointed. Callum talks a lot; Aguilar is a man of few words. Callum has nothing to live for; Aguilar is married to his duty. Callum has yet to discover a purpose for his life; Aguilar has embraced his heritage.

LEFT: Callum has spent much of his life in confinement, in contrast to the Assassins' emphasis on freedom.

TOP: Callum's artwork reveals the darkness of his mentality and hints to his ancestry.

"Callum saw something when he was a kid that no kid should see," Fassbender says. "So Callum is driven by violence, whereas Aguilar has a higher purpose." Much of Fassbender's energy in developing the script went into figuring out the relationship between the two characters, for the crux of the film lies in what Callum—and the audience—discovers that they have in common.

"Well, they do look alike," Fassbender quips. "Although, Aguilar has a beard. . . . Seriously, though, they are both stubborn, and they share a sense of loyalty, although Callum, like I said, doesn't really belong to anything. But when he does commit to somebody, or something, he is fiercely loyal to it."

As Jean de Rivieres points out, this is what makes the project "very, very human." Callum is on a journey to regain his humanity. Step by step, he starts to feel hope. Only his destiny is still cloaked in violence. It is this kind of moral complexity that makes the film so much more than an action movie.

"You understand what Michael's character is going through," says Frank Marshall, "and how, on the other side, he is going to come out a different person."

Visually there are interesting parallels drawn between the lethal injection equipment, with its vials of poison and plunging arms, and the biomechanical Animus to come. Set decorator Tina Jones based the design on what is currently in use in America (although New Mexico no longer has the death penalty), with a few stylistic alterations. "I don't think in reality the table forms a cross," she admits, referring to the fact that when Callum is strapped down his arms are outstretched as if on a crucifix. This not only references the Templar cross, it alludes to a Christ-like journey of death and resurrection.

ABOVE: Callum at first is only loyal to himself, but as the film progresses, he finds a new identity and purpose.

BELOW: Kurzel and Fassbender on set at the prison.

OPPOSITE: Aguilar is a master of multiple weapons.

INTO ABSTERGO

THE PRESENT DAY PARTS OF THE FILM are dominated by the futuristic headquarters of Abstergo, a research facility that is part of one of the largest multinational conglomerates in the world. "Ninety percent of the game is set in the past," Marshall says. However, 45 to 50 pages out of the 150-page film script take place in Abstergo. This emphasis required the company to be depicted in far greater detail than ever before. A mix of prison and mental institution, the mysterious complex held a much darker purpose than merely scientific research.

Ubisoft provided a detailed background for the corporation. Founded almost eighty years ago, it is primarily a front for the Templars. But most of its workforce remains oblivious to its secret identity. "We explain in the lore that Abstergo has separate divisions," Aymar Azaïzia says. "One

of them makes pharmaceuticals. We have research and development, as well as a historical division. And a videogame company, of course, like Ubisoft!"

Moreover, the Templars are not necessarily evil. They are endeavouring to better mankind. Through their work on DNA, they are striving for cures to cancer, autoimmune disease, and AIDS. According to their philosophy, order and discipline will result in true peace for humanity. "At the same time, if they find a way to become stronger and get rid of the Assassins, they will also do that," says Azaïzia.

In this particular enclave of Abstergo, the Templar agenda falls into the later category. Complex experiments are under way far from prying eyes. It is a cold place.

ABOVE: Overhead view of the Abstergo facility.

OPPOSITE BOTTOM: The crew preparing the Abstergo common room for filming.

ABOVE LEFT: Concept art of Callum running down the main corridor.

ABOVE RIGHT: Render of the hallway featuring the light pattern created by the honeycomb structure on the ceiling.

LEFT: Abstergo guards deploy to stop the patient rebellion.

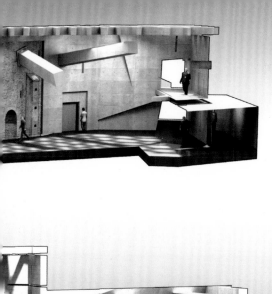

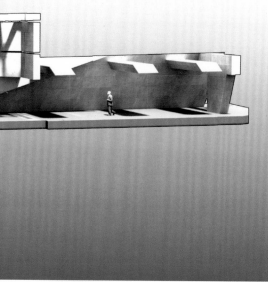

TOP LEFT: The stonewalls in the top image of the main corridor represent the outside of the Animus chamber. The walkway to the far left leads to Callum's cell.

TOP RIGHT: The main hallway creates a loop running over three hundred feet.

"When Justin talked about Abstergo, he was talking in terms of a museum, austere but with an elegant style," explains concept art director Virginie Bourdin. "But it was also sterile. It felt uncomfortable, more like a prison. There's no escape."

In terms of its basic architecture, Kurzel and Nicholson felt it important that Abstergo still bear the "brutalist, constructivist architecture" imagined for the game down to the same tri-part triangular logo. Days after he had signed on, Caroline Sol gave Nicholson a guided tour of Ubisoft's studio in Montreal, introducing him to the game designers, giving him a chance to grasp the fundamentals of the Assassin's Creed universe.

"Between meeting Justin, getting the job, and visiting Ubisoft, I watched clips of the game on YouTube." Nicholson exudes an air of expertise, a man who has literally thought through every inch of the movie. "You get very good insight into what the gamers enjoy about the game. And that was something to never forget."

What he took from his visit to Ubisoft and his own studies was how, wherever you found yourself in the game, there was always an escape route. So it was important to have that verticality incorporated into the sets. "In some of the bigger Abstergo sets there were double height spaces. You had a sense of space around them, because the game was like that." Having the sets rise high above the actors would draw the watcher's eye upward and hint of escape routes yet to be explored.

Nicholson masterminded a three-stage design process across all levels of the film, including both past and present. First, mood boards were created not only from his own studies, but the acres of research done by all his departments, including the detailed historical discoveries made by UMP.

Then, in discussion with Kurzel, he made preliminary sketches for all the principal settings and props, and depending on the technical requirements, they decided which department—be it art direction, set decoration, Bourdin's team of concept artists, or visual effects—would be responsible for which element.

Nicholson then rendered set designs in 3D software, a typical weapon in a modern filmmaker's arsenal. "It is much more efficient than pencil designs. Making cardboard models is good for meetings, but if you really want to show a director what a set is going to look like, use 3D." This was especially the case with the unusual spaces and shapes of Abstergo. The computer could then model the exact camera lens Kurzel might use, so he could get an immediate perspective of what the film would look like six months before it was shot. This enabled him to try out different lighting set ups and camera angles, to manipulate the space without the cost of building sets.

"When it came to Abstergo," Tina Jones says of their most complex set build, "Andy had a very clear idea of how it was going to be." Looking at the film as a whole, Abstergo embodied Nicholson's inclination to the clean and angular, whereas the cluttered, organic past epitomized Kurzel's tastes.

"The past is much more archaic, it's hotter and warmer and sweatier, it's got grit and texture," says the director, summing up the film's visual dichotomy. "Whereas Abstergo is much more architectural. There is definitely this kind of classical feel about it."

Fassbender, for one, relished the differences in the film's creative forces. "That is what you kind of want, isn't it?" he says. "That pull of opposites, who come together in the middle for great effectiveness."

"We were working towards the aesthetics of what the story needed," Nicholson says. Abstergo is a physical embodiment of the Templars' ethos. So Nicholson absorbed the angular features of the radical deconstructionist style (a sort of fragmentation of standard shapes). The dominance of glass and concrete, the angular geometry, matches the Templar philosophy, which Kurzel describes as "benign control." We can understand the Templars and their philosophy through their larger-than-life, sterile corporate headquarters.

"For me their desire to ultimately control free will makes it a very claustrophobic place to be. That is what I tried to do with the whole space." Nicholson describes a labyrinth of rooms that connect to a central corridor, like a spine that runs through the building, the only light available coming from high windows a patient could never hope to reach. "Even in the corridor that is almost 300-feet long, you never see the end of it. There is always another series of walls going off around the side. You can run as long as you want but you are never going to find a way out."

PREVIOUS PAGES: Concepts of the common room garden and surveillance room.

ABOVE: Although a sterile and uniform environment, each patient's cell shows hints of their personality.

OPPOSITE BOTTOM LEFT: Callum's ability to challenge the guards increases as he experiences more of Aguilar's skills.

OPPOSITE BOTTOM RIGHT: The hallway leading to the patient cells.

RIGHT: Callum fights the bleeding effect.

INTRODUCING SOFIA

CALLUM WAKES UP AFTER HIS FAILED EXECUTION and is greeted by the lovely face of Marion Cotillard's Sofia. Sofia will immediately present him with a second chance at a new life as a test subject for the Templars, who have a vested interest in his DNA.

Kurzel was eager to work with his *Macbeth* co-star again, because Cotillard would elevate the character of Sofia. "I thought that she would bring an effortless sophistication," he says, "and, in a sense, help elevate Abstergo, and what Abstergo meant."

Just as Callum is too complex to be classified as a straightforward hero, Sofia is by no means a villain. The head of the Animus program, she is a brilliant scientist with noble intentions. As Cotillard explains, "She has faith in science. She really thinks science can help humans become better humans. She truly believes that she is going find a cure to violence. It is the thing that drives her."

Despite working beneath the aegis of the Templars, Sofia is not necessarily swayed by the their philosophy. She really believes that she can eradicate violence and she hates the war between Assassins and Templars.

De Rivieres remembers attending the premiere of *Macbeth* and saying to Cotillard, "It must be weird, going from a Shakespeare adaption to a video game adaptation." But Cotillard's reply was serious, "You have no idea how much I love the world of *Assassin's Creed* and the themes in there."

Sofia's theory proposes that free will contains within it the root cause of violence. In altering, even removing, the gene responsible for free will, she can potentially eradicate war. Sofia has filled Abstergo with like-minded scientists bent on the same goal. She has also blinded herself to the fact that the halls of Abstergo are filled with the ghostly victims of past experiments. "The whole place is a paradox," says Cotillard.

With the Abstergo scenes filmed entirely in London, the French actress didn't begin until two months into production. But as soon as she arrived, Kurzel showed her five minutes of assembled Inquisition footage to give her an idea of what lay beyond the Animus. She was blown away. "It was

TOP LEFT: Cotillard and Kurzel in Callum's cell.

ABOVE: Although his jailor in a sense, Sofia wants to have Callum working with her voluntarily.

OPPOSITE BOTTOM: Renders of the recovery room, where patients recuperate after time in the Animus.

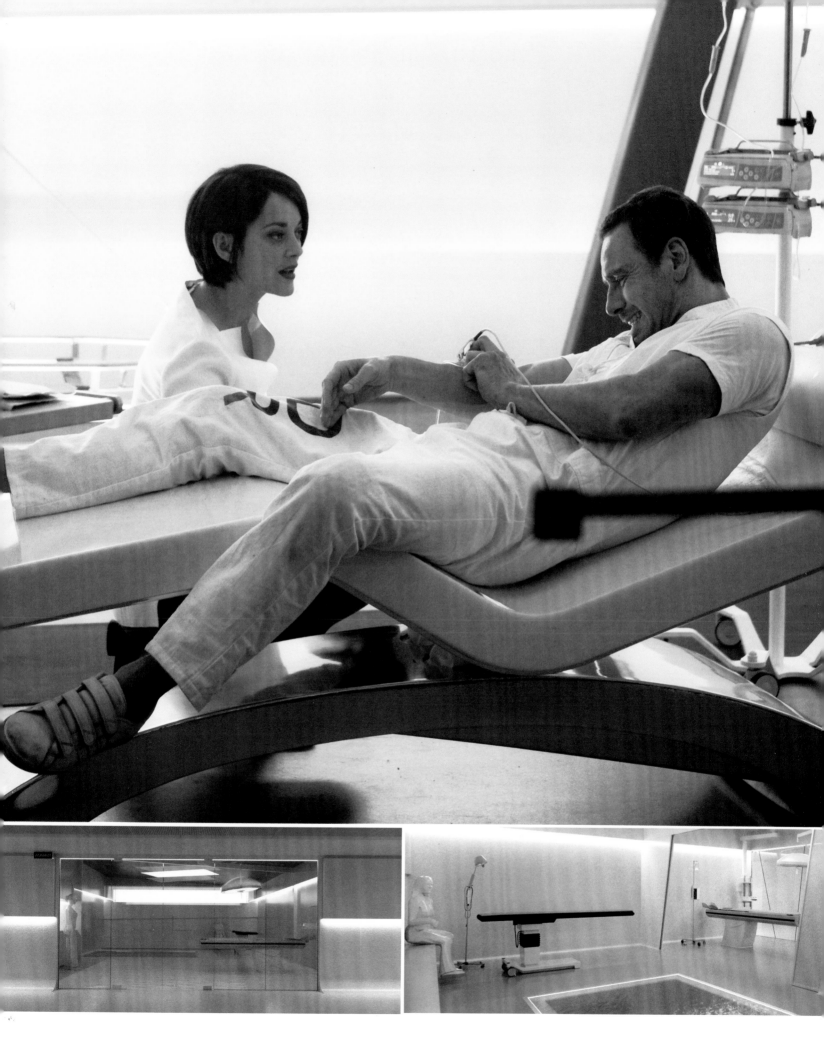

really spectacular. Justin was clearly as committed to this as he had been committed to *Macbeth*. But this was on a very different scale."

Through Callum's regression in the Animus, Sofia and the Templars finally hope to discover the whereabouts of a powerful artifact known as the Apple of Eden. The Apple contains a virtual map that pinpoints every trait on the human genome.

Sofia's interactions with Callum form the core relationship of the film. Each will transform the other. "With him, suddenly everything becomes possible," Cotillard says eagerly. "She is fascinated by the fact that she has found the right person, but also by the human being that he is. In her mind she thought he would be more of a binary person, if that makes sense. She discovers that he is not just this violent killer who was on death row. His soul is more full of light than darkness."

Such complexity is what impressed Cotillard about the material. Callum plants a seed in Sofia's mind, this nagging sense that she has been missing something. "She is a very, very sensitive person," she says, insistent Sofia is much more than the cliché of the cold-hearted intellectual. There is even an attraction to Callum. "At the beginning she really sees Callum as a lab rat, but she is fascinated by him. It is like a twisted attraction; it works on many levels. She is a very lonely person: She doesn't have a life besides her scientific quest. So it is very disturbing for her to be facing this beautiful and very human animal."

The CEO of Abstergo is Jeremy Irons' Alan Rikkin, Templar elder and Sofia's father. While he is the main antagonist in the film and a familiar figure from the games, Rikkin embodies some of the film's moral ambiguity. "He genuinely believes that society can be so much better if it is led and inspired by greater minds," Kurzel says. "He's about control, he's about making humanity evolve faster. So, there are certain aspects of his personality that are admirable, but essentially he is ruthless in his singular belief."

OPPOSITE TOP: A Templar shield in Alan Rikkin's collection.

OPPOSITE BOTTOM: Sofia's ambitions as a scientist place her in an interesting middle ground between villain and hero.

ABOVE: Rikkin's office contains many hidden treasures from throughout history.

BELOW: Sofia and her father's relationship is a civil, if not particularly affectionate, one.

FOLLOWING PAGES: Crusaders painting in the Abstergo conference room.

Tellingly, Rikkin's office is also the only room at Abstergo with a view. He is the only character in the movie with his own personal space, giving Nicholson the chance to represent a character through a physical environment and delve deeper into the Templar mind-set.

"His room is full of trophies that he has collected," Nicholson says. "It shows power, it shows reach, and it shows an excessive *collecting* of things. It says a lot about the historic standing of the Order—how long they have been around. It speaks of this search for the Pieces of Eden being something they have been undertaking for many years. And it speaks to him being the head of that, using all the powers that they have assembled to those ends."

Rikkin's office is a startling reliquary of both Templar and Assassin history. The glass cases are filled with items fans will recognize from the games. Bone mobiles reference the opening scenes in New Mexico. Jones is especially proud of Rikkin's desk, made of a checkerboard of American oak stained different colors to suggest the motif of chess—two sides locked in an eternal game.

Rikkin also happens to be Sofia's father, a troubled relationship that gives another slant on the idea of genetic heritage. How much is Sofia compelled to be like her father? Cotillard and Kurzel workshopped the idea that Sofia worships her father but hadn't spent a lot of time with him when she was young. "She probably chose to be a scientist to find a connection that would allow her to be close to him," Cotillard theorizes. "But her desire to reconnect with her father makes her totally blind."

Asked to sum him up, Cotillard describes Rikkin as "a warrior, a *cold* warrior."

EASTER EGGS

"Abstergo is filled with memories in glass cases and those memories are from the history of Assassin's Creed," says Brand Content Director Aymar Azaïzia. "One of them is the bow and arrow used by Connor in *Assassin's Creed III*. The chances are that you won't even notice it, but it's an example of the incredible detail in the film."

As a nod to the fans, director Justin Kurzel and his fellow filmmakers couldn't resist the opportunity to endow the film with specific references to the game. After all such "Easter Eggs" have been a popular feature of Assassin's Creed.

Kurzel confesses that he didn't even know what Easter Eggs were before the film. Not that it mattered—many of the references that he was told would excite fans were already things he had worked into the story. "So I am quite excited that a lot of that stuff doesn't feel as if it is

contrived," he says. "It doesn't feel as if it has been put in there as a treasure hunt, it is actually in there because of story."

Production designer Andy Nicholson explains that their Easter Eggs operate on two levels: more "on the nose" heavy references, and light references that will take a very sharp eye to discover.

The heavy references include items such as Assassin's weapons and the Pieces of Eden, and are frequently stored in the glass cabinets in the Animus Chamber and Rikkin's office

"It's meant to be things that the Templars have taken from the Assassins over the centuries," explains armourer Tim Wildgoose. "So Justin had us re-create weapons and cool things out of the games and then they were hidden in the background."

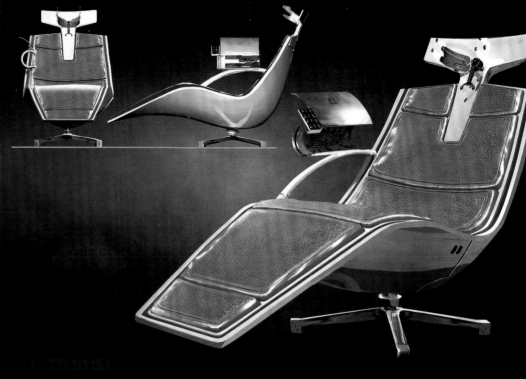

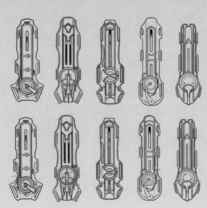

THESE PAGES: Treasures from Abstergo's vault and Rikkin's office include Connor's bow from *Assassin's Creed III*, various hidden blades dating back centuries, and an early version of the Animus.

FAR RIGHT: Concept of Ojeda's sword with a carving of Grand Master Hugues de Payens on the pommel.

For example, the cane sword that belongs to Jacob and Evie Frye from *Assassin's Creed: Syndicate* is encased in Rikkin's office along with a copy of the Codex, a book of Assassin lore written by Altaïr.

Light references come in a multitude of subtle forms. Will, for instance, you spot the Assassin's crest hidden among the Arabic lettering on the walls of the Alhambra? Or on the back of playing cards being dealt at Abstergo? As Nicholson points out, "There are Easter Eggs in Callum's prison cell and 1980s New Mexico that are very slight references: silhouettes, shapes, graffiti, things like that."

Set decorator Tina Jones had an avid gamer on her team who suggested references to the game that could be ingeniously slipped into the fabric of scenes. "A cart filled with hay is often important, so we put that in," says Jones.

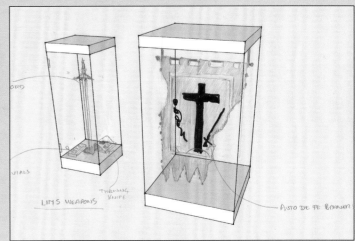

THE HIDDEN ASSASSINS

There is far more to the ghostly inmates who stalk the halls of Abstergo that initially meets the eye. As Callum comes to fulfil his destiny, so these background characters, previous subjects of Sofia's experiments with the Animus, reveal themselves to be members of the Assassin Brotherhood. Moreover, these particular Assassins are directly descended from some of the game's most famous characters, each with their own signature weapons. "We took the basic shapes and redesigned them with our own influence," explains armourer Tim Wildgoose, "but the essential designs of them are almost exactly like the games."

Emir (Matias Varela) is descended from Yusuf Tazim from *Assassin's Creed*: Revelations: "We just took the weapons straight out of the game. He has the eagle throwing knives on his shoulder," Wildgoose says. "He's got a very nice Islamic-influenced bow and arrow that we made for him. And he has Islamic-style wrist-blades."

Moussa (Michael K. Williams) is descended from Baptiste, a voodoo Assassin from *Assassin's Creed: Liberation*: "So he's got a bone voodoo spear," Wildgoose explains. "He has a voodoo-influenced wrist-blade which fires poison darts out. He has smoke bombs on a bandolier. He uses the Tiger Claw; that was something that I found in a book. It's something that Ninja used for hanging off the side of buildings for long

periods of time. It worked for Baptiste because it's a sort of African big cat tie-in."

Nathan (Callum Turner) is descended from Duncan Walpole from *Assassin's Creed IV: Black Flag*: "We made a very nice cutlass sword for him, which was taken straight out of the game. We also gave him this wrist crossbow, which is actually out of *Assassin's Creed: Unity*. It's like a bone wrist-crossbow. Everyone loved it so much conceptually that we decided to give it to him because we knew it would end up being seen prominently."

Linn (Michelle Lin) is descended from Shao Jun from *Assassin's Creed: Chronicles*: "She's the Chinese Assassin," says Wildgoose. "So she has a rope dart. It's like a throwing knife with a rope on it. Instead of wrist-blades, she has these shoes that have blades in them. She throws small needles. And she has a Jian Sword, which is a particular sort of Chinese sword."

ABOVE: In addition to his hand-to-hand combat skills, Emir also creates smoke bombs from materials in the common room garden.

OPPOSITE: Moussa, Linn, and Nathan with their signature weapons.

INSIDE THE LABYRINTH

HOUSED ON THE LEGENDARY 007 STAGE AT PINEWOOD, Abstergo wasn't a series of individual sets, but one giant, interlinked complex allowing Kurzel to mount long, fluid camera moves. One shot of Callum attempting to escape had Fassbender sprinting barefoot toward the camera from almost 100 feet away.

Marshall was amazed by the set's size. "It was huge! You could walk through, room to room. It just felt *real*."

According to Nicholson's calculations, the giant set gave the director "230 feet of travel to go through and around rooms." He loved that you got a sense of how the rooms joined together—this big, sculpted, angular space. It even began to work symbiotically with the script, as sequences were adapted for their new spaces.

"The common room became the surveillance room," Nicholson says by way of example. As written, it was fifteen pages of security guards looking at monitors, which wasn't terribly exciting from a visual perspective. In one interwoven set, they could fuse it with the common room. So not only could the guards observe the whole complex via screens, they could look directly in on the inmates via a glass wall. "It was very theatrical," Nicholson explains, "It was a direct imposition on the patients' freedom."

ABOVE: The Infinity Room set.

OPPOSITE TOP: Actor Michael K. Williams as Moussa.

RIGHT: Concept of the Abstergo rooftop garden.

Their largest dramatic departure from the game, de Rivieres was fascinated by what he calls the "alchemy" of Abstergo. He found that the company's labyrinthine headquarters radiated a very current paranoia over corporate power and manipulation. "We explored the hidden agendas of this massive corporation," he says. "With people locked away in a facility like this, and a scientist with a vision and an ego, trying to change the world—that's fascinating.

"Everybody sees the whole spectacle in the past with Aguilar," he continues, "but personally I am also excited about the modern world. The modern day facility will *breathe* into the past. The mix between the two periods is what makes the movie special."

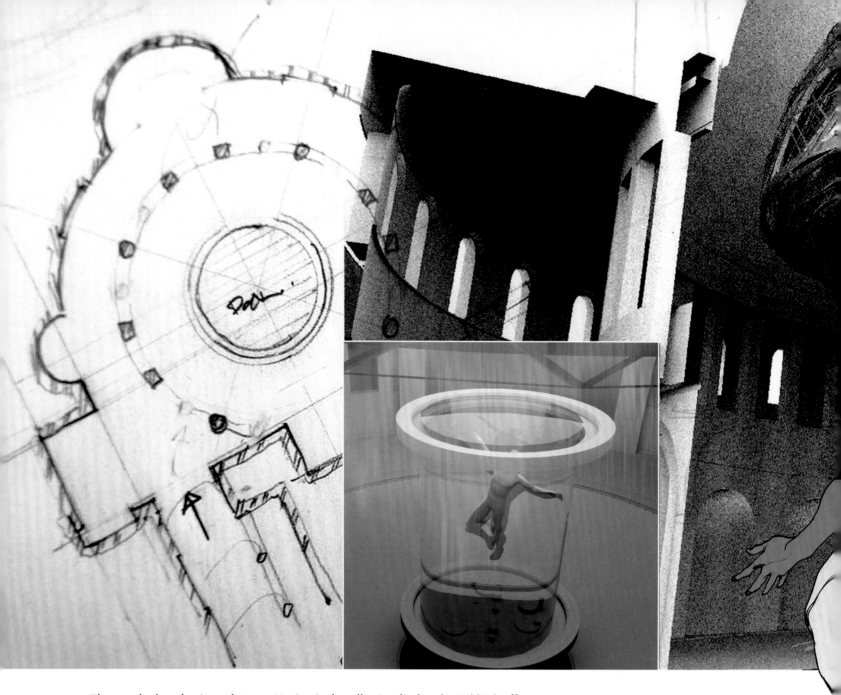

The past also breathes into Abstergo. Not just in the collection displayed in Rikkin's office, but also in the tree that Jones placed along the endless corridor, at the base of which are seemingly innocuous stones. Inscribed into each of them—barely within range of the camera—are ancient prayers. For the spacious common room, the set decorator found a French designer who made small, futuristic aquariums—angular, glass boxes with plants sprouting from the top. "We made our own," she explains, "so in the common room, we had eels and piranhas swimming in these aquariums." The eels echo the eel merchants in old Spain; the piranhas suggest something more predatory.

A combined corporate facility, laboratory, museum, prison, and asylum, Abstergo also possesses the sanctified mood of a cathedral. At its heart lies the Animus Chamber: a huge, vaulted room—the largest single interior in the film—containing the advanced technology of the Animus, through which Callum will regress into the realms of his genetic memory. The very gateway to the past, the design of the chamber is a literal fusion of the old and new. An ancient stonewall encircles the Animus with a mosaic floor beneath, evidence that the sleek, modern building has been built around the remnants of an old church.

ABOVE LEFT: The first drawing of the Animus Chamber created for the film.

ABOVE MIDDLE: An early model of the Animus had Callum immersed in a tank of water.

OVERLAY: Sketch exploring the Animus arm.

ABOVE RIGHT: Early concept of the Animus.

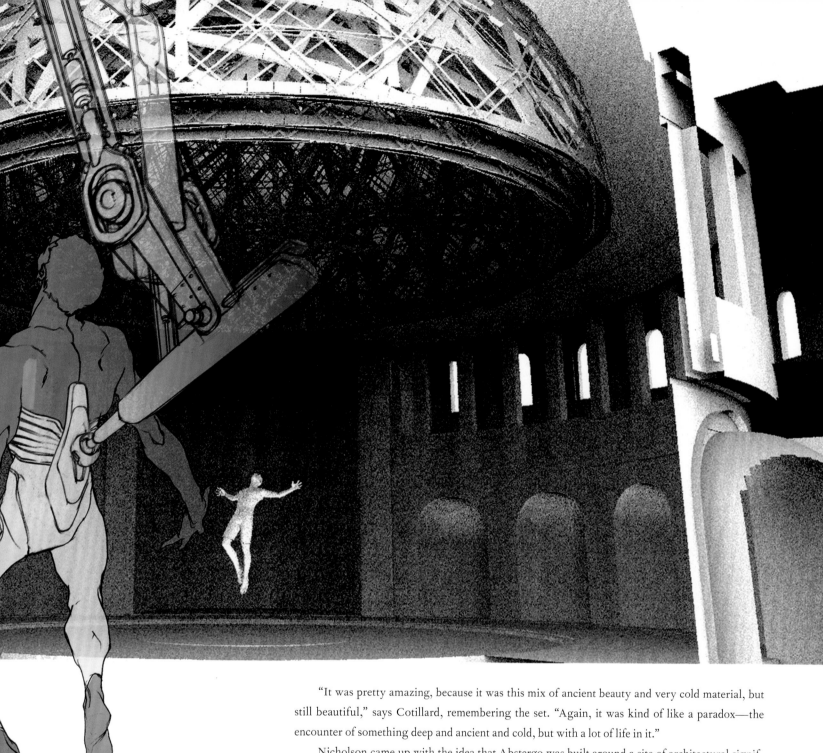

"It was pretty amazing, because it was this mix of ancient beauty and very cold material, but still beautiful," says Cotillard, remembering the set. "Again, it was kind of like a paradox—the encounter of something deep and ancient and cold, but with a lot of life in it."

Nicholson came up with the idea that Abstergo was built around a site of architectural significance to the Templars, *and* possibly sacred to the Assassins. "So we made it this Byzantine space. I like Byzantine architecture—it is almost Roman. I felt very strongly it should be a church, something even older than Aguilar. It is eleventh or twelfth century compared to the fifteenth century. It has a beautiful mosaic floor, which is almost Roman, with a big Templar cross in it."

It also served a more practical visual purpose. Kurzel and Nicholson found it was too jarring to cut directly between the fury and excitement of the fifteenth century and the muted, claustrophobic concrete hive of Abstergo.

The Animus Chamber is a transitional space, and the heart of the film. Here the past and present will overlap, as the terrifying Animus delves into Callum's DNA. Here the process of his evolution into an Assassin will take place. Callum, through his ancestor and the past, discovers who he is. "It is through the Animus," the director says, "that he learns where he comes from."

CHAPTER 3

THE ANIMUS

THE ULTIMATE VIRTUAL REALITY

"THIS REALLY WAS THE MAIN CHALLENGE," says Michael Fassbender. "How do we make something organic out of a machine? How can we show more than Callum just sitting in a chair? How could we impress the game development team with what we came up with? Well, we definitely achieved all of that."

The film's most daring evolution of Assassin's Creed mythology, the Animus is the advanced virtual reality technology that allows operators to access the genetic memory of a subject and replay it to them as if was happening there and then. According to the game's theory, the entire life history of our ancestors is stored in our genes, and the Animus locates a particular ancestor and zeroes in on a particular time.

Naturally, the Animus was going to be central to any proposed movie version of the game. After all, this is the means by which the present bridges with the past. However, the game iteration was fairly static. "Get into a chair, put on the VR goggles, and get into the past," Aymar Azaïzia says. "We needed more drama and more physicality."

Indeed, Kurzel was insistent on something far more visual than having someone prone on a chair with a few sensors attached to their head. Or even the futuristic dentist's chair in *The Matrix*, where the VR connection is made via an invasive cable.

Kurzel wanted something completely original, and tasked Nicholson and his team to envisage a technology both otherworldly and plausible. "In the game, because you spend so much time in the past, the Animus is a modern day vehicle to get you into those elements," the director explains. "Whereas in the film, the contemporary side became the real driving force, so the Animus had to be a kind of machine that felt dangerous. It had to have the ability to teach Callum how to be an Assassin, not just psychologically but physically."

ABOVE AND OPPOSITE TOP: Concepts of how the arm connects to the chamber roof.

BELOW: Early concept of the Animus Chamber.

OPPOSITE BOTTOM: Stunning concept of the light display created by the Animus.

METAL

TRANSLUCID PLASTIC

TENDONS

The development of the new Animus would focus all the various levels of creative thinking that had gone into the film as a whole: Kurzel's gritty vision, Andy Nicholson's precision-tooled approach, a marriage of computer effects and practical sets, the stunt team's inexhaustible prowess, and, of course, Fassbender's astonishing physical talents. Their Animus was to be something truly cinematic and terrifying.

The Animus is a snakelike extension going into the spine. Callum is suspended in the Animus and starts to live what his ancestor is doing. As Aguilar fights and climbs and leaps, so Callum, trapped in his memories, will enact the very same moves. When Aguilar leaps from a building, the arm of the Animus matches the move by plunging Callum towards the floor.

Kurzel elaborates, "The Animus is set up like a theater, with Callum at the center. The past is displayed through light projections overlaid onto the present, almost like holograms or ghosts, which are recorded by Abstergo so they can be replayed later. For example, when Aguilar fights a Templar in the past, I can cut back to Callum who is fighting a memory version, an expressionistic version of that Templar."

If Aguilar is climbing a wall, we will see Callum climbing a wall made of light. The arm is helping him move up, but you see the architecture of the wall that allows him to imagine that he is actively involved in the actions of Aguilar in fifteenth-century Spain.

OPPOSITE TOP: Animus arm studies.

OPPOSITE BOTTOM: Two orderlies connect Callum to the Animus.

TOP LEFT: Wires and rigging were used to mimic the arm during filming.

ABOVE: Exploration of the arm details.

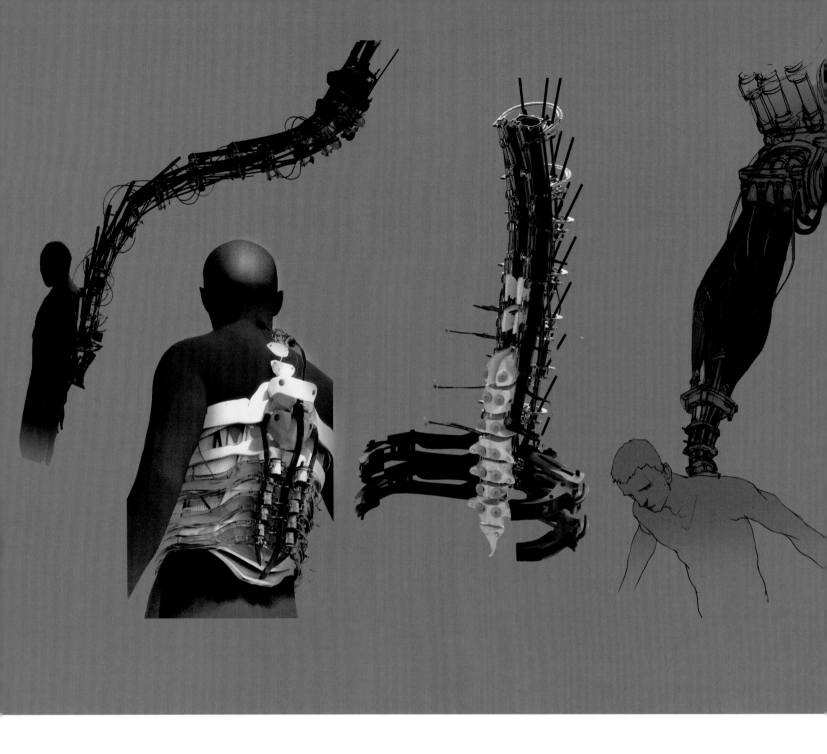

EVOLUTION OF THE ANIMUS

THE IMMEDIATE CHALLENGE FOR THE DESIGN TEAMS was how to create an Animus that allowed us to feel what Callum was going through as he achieves "synchronicity" (the integration of subject and Animus) with the past. If he were simply prone in a chair, the effect would be reduced to flickering eyelids and twitching limbs, the kind of subconscious tremors that have been done before.

The conduit of all the Animus development, concept artist advisor Virginie Bourdin was brought on by Nicholson to help create concept art for *Assassin's Creed*. Having worked as a "VFX concept artist" on over thirty films, Bourdin saw her role as fundamentally "understanding the visual language Nicholson wanted to create." And given his ultra-detailed approach and use of 3D modeling techniques, she was soon heading up an entire team of artists, a bridge between the production department and special effects.

THESE PAGES: Creating the Animus arm.

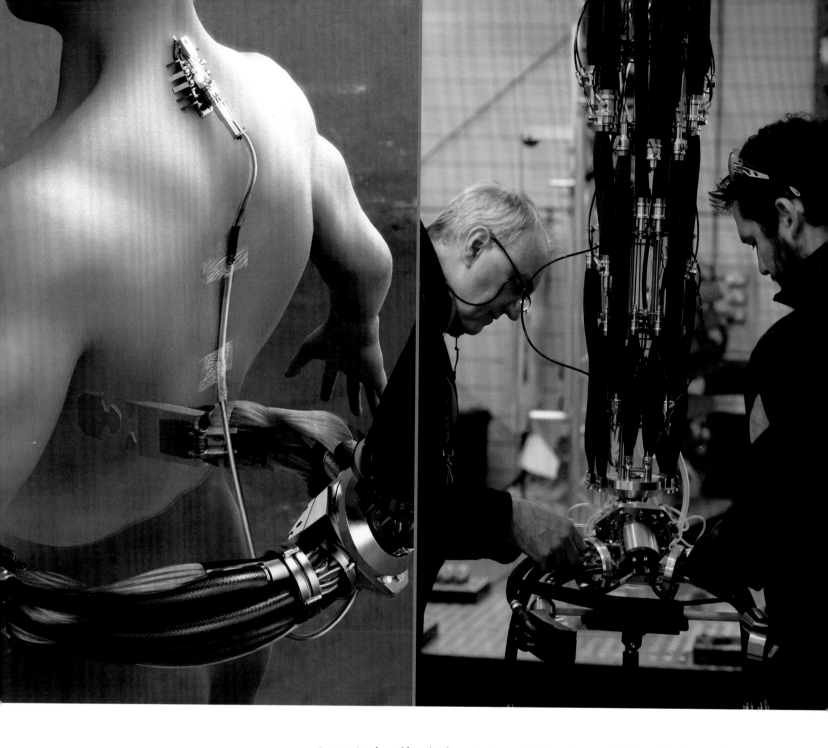

Immersing herself in the four gigabytes of information provided by Ubisoft, Bourdin's role has focused on conceptualizing the "iconic props": among them the Apple of Eden and the Animus.

She sums up her mission in simple terms. "My job is to put all of the choices in front of Justin and Andy so they can decide what is the most important."

Early versions of the script had suggested plunging Callum into a pool of water. "You've got to think about security," Bourdin says. "You're talking about submerging Michael Fassbender."

Nicholson was unconvinced of the visual interest of a tank of water. So Bourdin reduced the tank to a cylinder full of water, wherein Callum would be placed on some kind of submerged seat. Then Nicholson thought it would be interesting if Callum were lowered into the water on an extending robotic arm. This was their eureka moment. Once you had the arm, there was no need for the water.

"That's when we started to do these drawings," Bourdin recalls, "and Justin said, 'Oh, *that's* interesting.'"

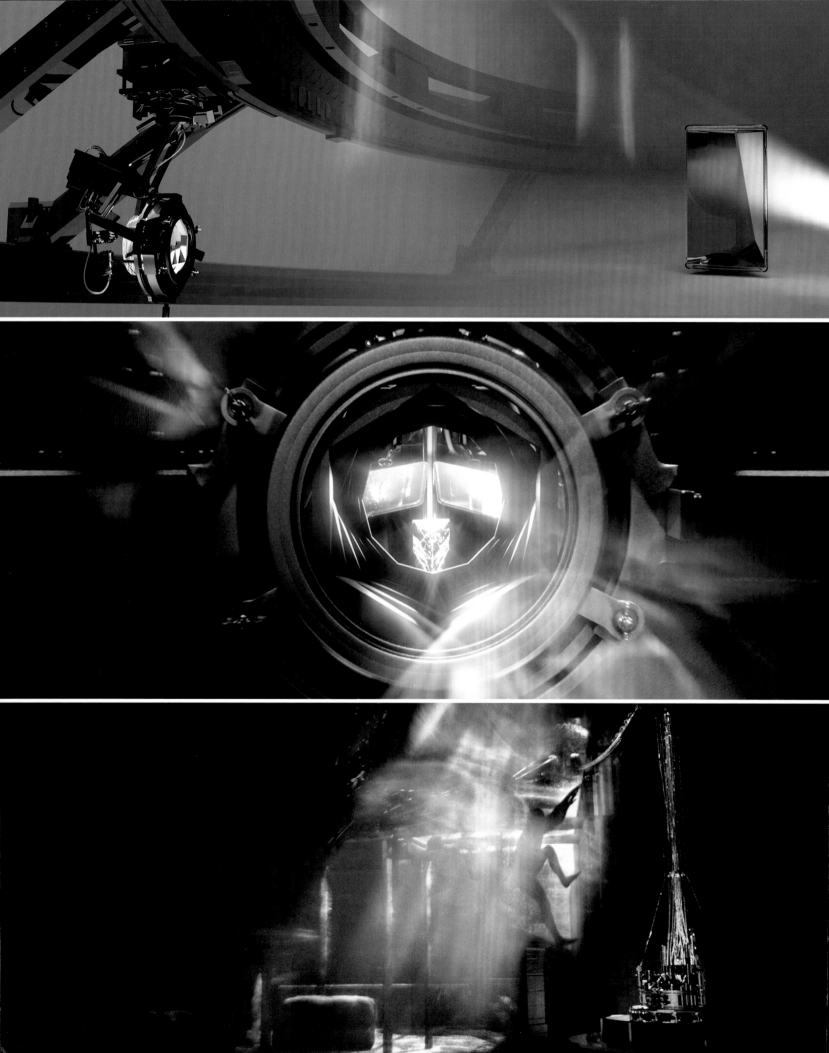

OPPOSITE TOP AND MIDDLE: The machine that creates the light projections.

OPPOSITE BOTTOM: Example of how the Animus projects human figures into the chamber.

THIS PAGE: Concept artists overlaid images on top of the film stills to gauge how the light projections would appear in the final version.

FOLLOWING PAGES: Bleeding effect concepts.

Straightaway the director saw how being mounted on the end of Animus arm allowed the actor to be far more expressive. His medium would be the air—not water—and the practicality of the idea appealed to Kurzel's background in theater.

Bourdin then began focussing on how dance and theater performances sometimes use video in a stage environment, and the inkling of another idea formed in her head. During a subsequent meeting she suggested, "Maybe we can have him surrounded by the imagery from the past."

The Animus projects these apparitions of Aguilar in the fifteenth century, whose movements would be matched a split-second later by Callum. "It becomes a kind of dance between the contemporary and the historical," Kurzel says.

Nicholson describes it as a feedback loop. "You are connected by an epidural to the machine that reads your past, processes the information, then plays back the information to your central nervous system. If you're running along the floor or climbing a wall, it feeds back to your muscles. When Aguilar fights, you will physically see Callum move as if he were hitting stuff. If he is climbing up a church wall, you will see that represented for the onlooker."

"What Callum sees appears in the Animus room," Frank Marshall adds, "so the scientists can see what is going on inside his head projected around the room. It is a really complicated editing issue."

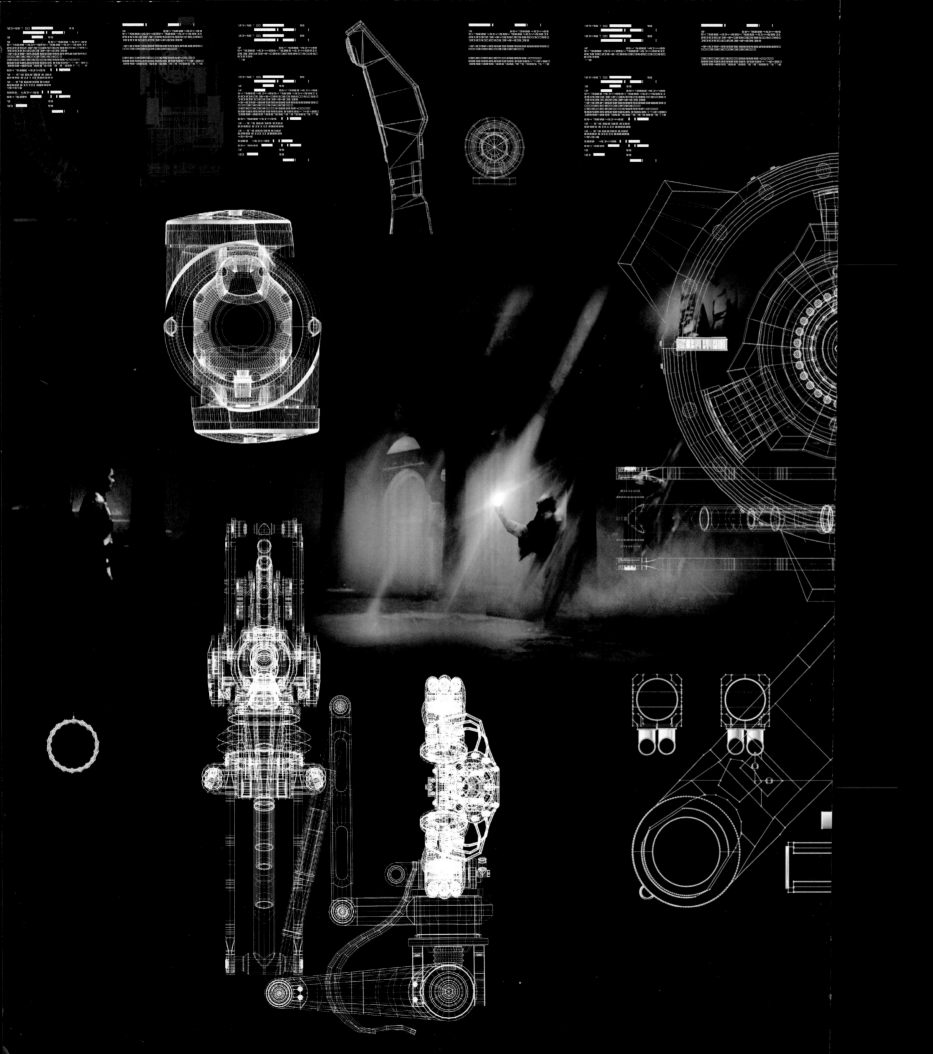

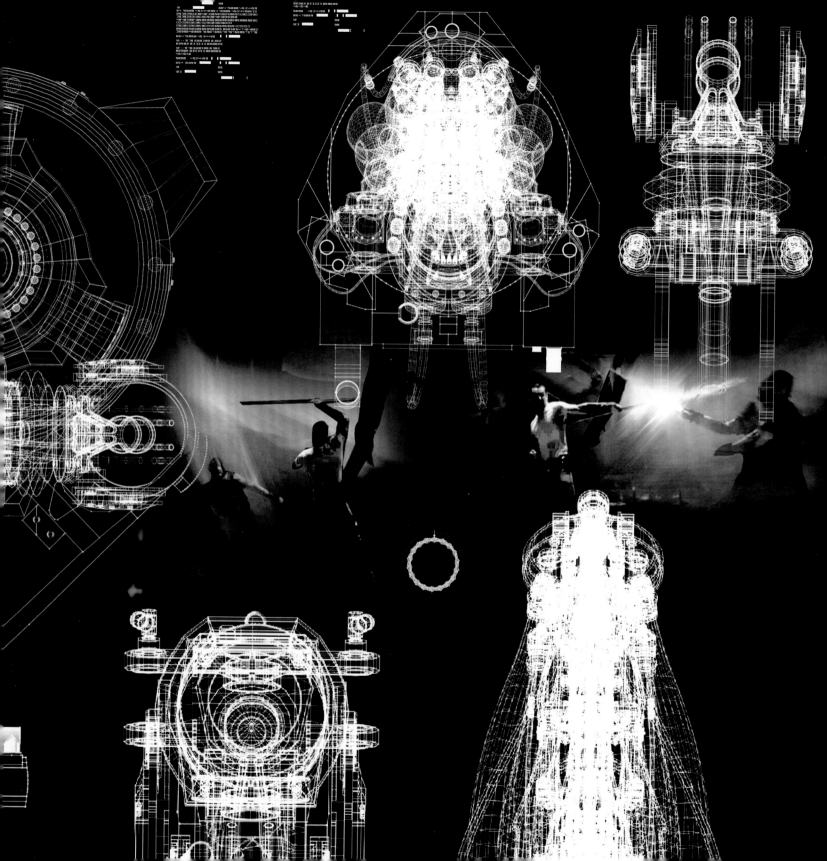

A LIVING MACHINE

AS WELL AS FUSING PAST AND PRESENT, the design of the Animus machine itself embodies the intertwining of the aesthetics of Kurzel and Nicholson. Both approaches, Bourdin says, have a great purity—and together they created one voice. For this robotic tentacle or arm would be envisaged both as a machine and something forbiddingly organic.

Nicholson began with straightforward robotics. "It had to feel real," he says. "Real is a big thing for Justin. It is a big thing for me too. You really believe the arm is moving." He came up with the idea of inverting a six-axis motion rig, which is the base for flight simulators, out of which extended the arm.

After seeing his production designer's functional approach, Kurzel wanted to synthesise it with a biological texture. The Animus should feel strange and discomforting. Nicholson added a system of pneumatic muscles to give it "character."

Fundamental to Kurzel's thinking was the idea of the dance—the machine is not pulling the subject around and the subject is not pulling the arm around. The interaction was to be very subtle, this almost imperceptible tug of war over who was leading. It would seem as if the Animus was almost conscious.

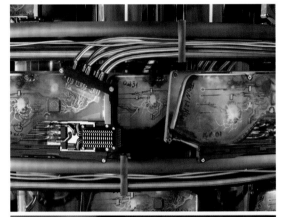

Through his three regressions Callum learns to control the flow of memories: barely keeping up with them at first, but by the second regression, both partners would be in tune, and then in the third he would move ahead of the Animus as if predicting its signals. "Eventually he's motivated," Bourdin says, "and he goes faster than the machine."

The resulting vision of man entwined with machine, fashioned in CGI, is something that wouldn't look out of place in a horror movie. As Bourdin describes it, the biomechanical equipment would be "all body without skin." She elaborates, "like something coming back from the dead."

"I really saw it as kind of an animal that allows you to be connected to ancient blood," says Marion Cotillard. "This vehicle of blood and DNA and all this complexity that lives inside a human being."

At the end of the arm, Callum will be held fast by a titanium "ribcage," from which a needle will snake its way into his back, forming an epidural, and begin the process of extraction. As Azaïzia puts it, "The Animus will be plugged directly into his backbone."

Once they had a working concept for the arm, Bourdin turned her thoughts to depicting how the central unit—the body of the Animus—would operate. Maintaining the concept of a biological machine—and to compliment the organically rooted concept of DNA memory—Kurzel envisaged it as the brain to which the spine was still attached. Bourdin likens its eventual look to a brain pickled in formaldehyde.

"I think we have done a brilliant job with that," says Nicholson. "The whole technology around reading memories is organic, with chemicals and spores rather than digital data. The way we interface with that is kind of molecular interface."

Memories are drawn out of the subject's DNA while he relives them as if they were real, fed up the umbilical arm, and imprinted as organic matter, which then crystallises and is made into a memory card. "We proposed this would give an electrical impulse to every muscle," Bourdin recalls, "but this was difficult to envisage with Callum covered by his inmate costume."

All their ideas had to be tested not just against Kurzel's conviction that his world had to be convincing, but against the more pragmatic realities of costumes, props, special effects, and production design: what aided storytelling . . . and what inhibited it. Ultimately, they concentrated on the ebb and flow of memory through the arm and how it attached to the spinal cord. As Bourdin sanguinely puts it, "being medically correct."

TOP: Memory core concepts.

MIDDLE AND BOTTOM: Animus console concepts.

OPPOSITE: Render of the Animus machine.

ANIMUS SUBJECT DNA ANALYSIS REPORT

TO BE FILLED IN BY EXAMINING PHYSICIAN *(please print)*

Name: Callum Lynch

| **Date and place of birth:** Alcalde NM, 21 Oct 1979 | **DNA pattern:** G.83b | **Age:** 37 |

37.4 C / 99.3 F
37.2 C / 98.9 F
36.9 C / 98.5 F
36.7 C / 98.0 F

36.1 C / 97.0 F

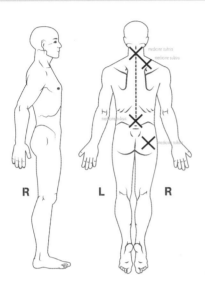

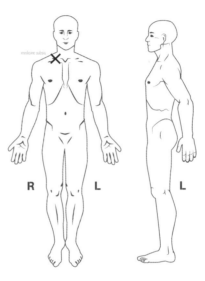

R   L   R   R   L   L

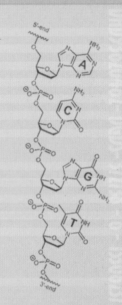

5'-end
A
C
G
T
3'-end

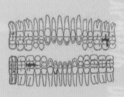

	Yes	No		Yes	No		Yes	No		Yes	No
Measles			Shortness of Breath			Rheumatic Fever/Heart Murmur			Head Injury with Unconsciousness		
German Measles			Gallbladder Trouble/Gallstones								
Mumps			Hepatitis			Rupture, Hernia			High or Low Blood Pressure		
Tuberculosis			Recent Gain/Loss of Weight			Disease or Injury of Joints or Back					
Arthritis			Pain/Pressure in Chest						Blood Clotting Disorder		
Epilepsy, Convulsions			Anemia			Tumor, Cancer, Cysts			Urinary Tract Condition Kidney/Bladder		
Asthma, Hay Fever			Palpitations (Heart)			Alcohol Consumption					
Eye Disease			Weakness, Paralysis			Sickle Cell Disease or Trait			Stomach/Intestinal Trouble/Ulcers		
Smoker			Stroke								
Ear/Nose/Throat Trouble			Dizziness, Fainting			High Cholesterol					

A. Are you currently under the care of a physician?	Surgeries - List	Allergies – Drugs or other
B. Are you taking any medication for heart disease or high blood pressure?		
C. Are you currently taking any other prescription medication on a routine basis?		

Gynecological History	Yes	No		Yes	No		Yes	No
Is this First Pap			Pain during Intercourse			Severe Cramps/Pain during Period		
History of STDS			Breast Disease			Pelvic Infections (Uterus/Tubes/Ovaries)		
Abnormal Bleeding			Cancer			Have Period Every Month		
Age Periods Began:				Abnormal Pap:				
Duration of Period:				Treatment:				
Birth Control Methods Used::				Other:				

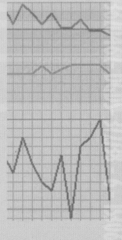

_____
PRINTED NAME OF LICENSED PHYSICIAN

DANCING WITH THE PAST

CALLUM'S THREE REGRESSIONS TAKE HIM to three different locations in Aguilar's present. But it's a risky process. There is the "bleeding effect." The more time someone spends in the Animus, the more likely it is their ancestor's mental make-up will spill over into their psyche, potentially causing instability, or "desynchronization." It can kill or mentally destroy a patient.

Azaïzia elaborates, "There are some positive aspects, such as you're probably going to be able to start doing some parkour. But at the same time, you're also going to have a lot of mental trouble or a heart attack, because your body is not ready for that level of strain. There's a reason why a lot of people who have been in the Animus look catatonic."

Thus the film becomes a race against time—can Sofia extract the right memory and locate the Apple of Eden before Callum is left a ghost like the other inmates? Or, indeed, will Callum's Assassin's lineage allow him to overcome, even embrace, the bleeding effect?

Paradoxical though it sounds, Callum needed the freedom to mimic all that Aguilar is doing while attached to the machine. So to "validate the integrity" of the concept, Bourdin studied the signature fighting and freerunning moves of the Assassins. She met with the experts at Ubisoft responsible for animating the martial arts techniques and had her team do their own animations to get a sense for the constraints of the machine. It was a finely balanced equation. "How much should it help the movement of the actor," she posits, "or constrain the movement of the actor?"

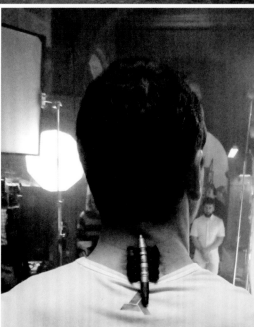

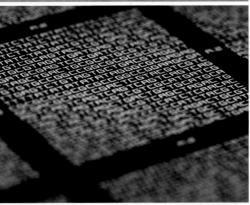

OPPOSITE TOP: Michael Fassbender filming in the Animus Chamber.

OPPOSITE BOTTOM: The epidural prop.

TOP LEFT: Two crewmembers developing the arm puppet.

TOP RIGHT: Through the Animus, Callum will experience Aguilar's actions five hundred years in the past.

ABOVE: Monitor graphics.

In order to re-create Aguilar's movements, the Animus sequences needed to be filmed towards the end of the shoot. For Fassbender and his stunt double there was not only the physical challenge of mimicking their own footsteps, but also the challenge of expressing Callum's subtle progression as he learns from Aguilar. Stunt master Ben Cooke needed to figure out how to replicate moves they had completed weeks ago on location in Malta and Spain. Moreover those stunts couldn't be mirror images of one another; he needed to instil them with subtle learning process that enables Callum to match Aguilar's skills. "He's getting closer and closer and closer until they become one kind of thing," Cooke explains. "Until Callum and Aguilar actually sort of blend. So there's a journey in Callum's physicality."

While on location they chose specific pieces of action for Callum to mirror as the film cuts back and forth between Abstergo and the Inquisition. Once back at Pinewood, Cooke carefully plotted which of their chosen mirror-moves came from which regression, reinterpreting each part of the dance based on the three skill levels Callum has gradually gained from his experiences as Aguilar.

"Towards the end where Callum is becoming more like Aguilar," Kurzel says, "we start to intercut quite seamlessly between the two. In a sense Aguilar and Callum become one."

To re-create the motions of the Animus on set, Fassbender and his stunt-double were suspended on wires with a visual effects tracking point on their back. The actor would begin and finish a particular sequence in the Animus, and depending on the complexity or risks inherent in the move, his place was taken by either stuntmen or digital replacements.

Even though the Animus arm would be fully digital, both Kurzel and Nicholson were determined to create a real reference to work from. Without the time to construct a complete version of the arm, Nicholson had a "marionette" of the lower section of the arm constructed. Operated by the crew, the arm pulsates as it moves, as if it were breathing. Bourdin laughs, "It's like the puppet arm is acting."

The look and supple movements of the Animus would continue to be refined throughout the postproduction period, but the concept so impressed the programmers at Ubisoft that they hope to adopt it into future versions of the Assassin's Creed game. A feedback loop has been created: out of the game into the movie and back into the game again.

EAGLE VISION

WHENEVER CALLUM—AND THE AUDIENCE—makes the leap into the skin of Aguilar, there is a significant transitional phase where we first view events through the eyes of an eagle. This eagle-vision could be a mystical Assassin talent. Or it could easily be symbolic. Or just a stylish exposition shot before the film focuses in on Aguilar's storyline. Ask and you'll get numerous intriguing explanations.

Kurzel defines the eagle as a "guardian angel."

Marshal believes it is a forewarning. "But it also gives us the ability to lead the camera in from the present, a transitional element taking us into the world."

There is a sequence when the eagle alights in a tree. As the camera follows the tree downwards, we see Aguilar drop to the ground as if the eagle has just transformed into a human.

"It started out as a tool in our game." Azaïzia, with his extensive knowledge of the franchise, has a detailed explanation. "You've probably seen that there's a lot of references to the iconography of the eagle. When you look at our characters, it's a metaphor for the way they move, leaping from rooftop to rooftop, mimicking the eagle."

Within the game, whenever a character is about to make a Leap of Faith, you can hear the cry of an eagle. Azaïzia sees it as the incarnation of an Assassin's free will. The Assassin, he says, is like an eagle, looking for his prey in the middle of a crowd. Little wonder the motif of the eagle has been incorporated into all the Assassin costumes and names.

"In the franchise, every single character's name is a derivative of a bird of prey," Azaïzia explains. "Ezio is 'eagle' in Italian."

The name Aguilar comes from the Spanish "aguila" meaning "eagle." During the final regression, as Callum embraces his heritage, an eagle can be seen circling the Animus Chamber and finally passing into Callum. It is the soul of Aguilar being accepted by his descendant.

OPPOSITE: The eagle is an important symbol in the Assassin's Creed universe. The Leap of Faith even embodies the physical structure of an eagle.

TOP: Artwork of a Moorish fortress where Aguilar is initiated into the Assassin Brotherhood.

CHAPTER 4

THE INQUISITION

CRUEL THEATER

THE MOORISH SPLENDOR OF THE ALHAMBRA, with its complex of palaces and mosaics, has presided over Granada since the year 889. Yet most of the citizens know nothing about its hidden tunnels. Buried beneath the treasured historical site lies a maze of narrow passages, and it was here Caroline Sol found herself with a lamp on her forehead, caked in dust, spiders in her hair, crawling along the ground. "Like in an Indiana Jones movie!" she says proudly. However, her thoughts were focused on *Assassin's Creed*. She remembers that as she crept on her hands and knees beneath the palaces of the Moors filming had already begun in another part of Spain. Nevertheless, these tunnels would end up in the script. Having rescued the Apple of Eden from Torquemada's clutches, Aguilar needed an exit plan from the Alhambra. And history itself had provided the answer.

After the spare, geometric spaces of Abstergo, the Inquisition was to feel like a blast of life in all its spectacular, and often horrifying, detail. It had to live up to Fassbender's description of a "cruel theater."

"If we were going to set the present in an Abstergo that was very stark," says the actor, "the regressions would need to be a very different visual experience."

"It was a chance to do the grit and texture and also be flamboyant," Andy Nicholson says. "The game is quite theatrical when it comes to representing the past, so we needed to have fun."

For Justin Kurzel there were a variety of inspirations for how he wanted to portray the past. He felt the vivid contrasts of light and dark in Caravaggio's paintings served the idea of the Assassins working by stealth and being able to quickly disappear into darkness. "It has a slightly film noir quality to it," he says.

By contrast, he was also inspired by Sergio Leone's Westerns for their big wide-angled vistas and *Lawrence of Arabia* where real light was being captured by the camera. "Light is a huge motif in *Assassin's Creed*," the director explains, "and that influences the visuals. And then it was just trying to make everything real."

According to Kurzel, the present is blue and gray like a bruise, and the past is very yellow and orange like fire. "As if everything takes place at either dusk or early morning," he says. "You can see and feel the dust and smoke in the air. It is not clean; there is no blue sky."

Nicholson put a lot of research not only into fifteenth-century paintings, but fifteenth-century paint, upholding the principal of historical veracity. At that time purple dyes simply did not exist, and outside of Venice, blue was very rare in Europe.

With Granada and Seville now bustling, modern cities, they would need to re-create the urban landscape of 1491 elsewhere. Malta, in particular its relatively well-preserved capital of Valletta, offered the ideal canvas on which to envisage the turbulent Inquisition. When Nicholson glanced across the rooftops, the clutter of church towers and battlements was a vision of antiquity. He appreciated how Valletta sits on a "spit of land" that juts out into the sea and has become heavily weathered. The sandstone crumbles easily.

"A film like this is a world building exercise; you are going into the fifteenth century, but it's a fifteenth century with very specific events, a very grand period," he says. "I had to find Malta locations that would become a version of Seville that isn't exactly what Seville would have been like, but has all the notes, tropes, and motifs that would work for what we are doing in the film."

Frank Marshall, who has had his fair share of experience mounting stunts in sweltering locations from his Indiana Jones days, was impressed with what the Mediterranean island offered. "It has such a good infrastructure there already," he says. "You get great production support, and we

OPPOSITE TOP: Set decoration of a Seville street.

OPPOSITE BOTTOM: Aguilar against the backdrop of a modern Spanish city.

TOP: Aguilar drops into the hidden tunnels beneath the Alhambra.

needed a lot of extras. But mostly these historical monuments are unchanged. And the government is pretty kind to movies. Unless the site is very fragile, you can shoot where you want." Even if what you had in mind was to climb up the walls and dangle from window ledges.

Indeed, they made quite a spectacle. "We had ten cranes on a set," the producer says. "Some for set build, some for rigging, some for lighting. We often shot in very low light levels, and you had to supplement that."

For Nicholson nothing beats how good locations open up the filmmaking process. "Valletta gave us some great vistas, including a shot from a 60-foot-high cathedral looking down to the ground. If you just built a set, you wouldn't necessarily think of doing something like that. It forces you to deal with a lot of problems, but it also forces you make the scale grander than it would have been."

ABOVE: A street in Malta transformed into a fifteenth-century Seville market.

OPPOSITE TOP: Set decorators re-created a historically accurate kitchen for the auto-de-fé chase scene.

OPPOSITE MIDDLE: Set decoration of a nobleman's house.

OPPOSITE BOTTOM: Granada and its surrounding landscape feature a red, dusty color palette.

Malta also served as a base for building massive Inquisition-era sets such as their re-creation of the Alhambra's Court of Lions, and the auto-da-fé, which included 800 extras for the crowd. Nicholson, who had shot *Troy* in Malta twelve years before, appreciated how it forced a certain scale on what they achieved. "It demanded to be slightly grandiose."

While background plates would be shot in Granada and Seville, the landscape around Almeria provided the terrain for the carriage chase and the early New Mexico scenes. The most arid place in Europe, bounded to the north by desert, Almeria has movie history written into its DNA. David Lean shot sequences from *Lawrence of Arabia* here, and this is the backdrop for Sergio Leone's Spaghetti Westerns; two of Kurzel's touchstones for *Assassin's Creed*.

"With Aguilar we wanted to explore that Western idea of a hero that doesn't speak that much." Fassbender acknowledges they are tipping their hat to Clint Eastwood's legendary Man With No Name. "He is very much about the action."

If Malta and Almeria provided the setting and golden climate, it was then the job of the various departments to bring the foreground of history to life. Production design would seamlessly adjust and extend the sets, building extra layers, and providing concealed handholds and ledges for the stuntmen to use.

Then set decoration would move in to fill a location with the paraphernalia of the age, shipping over props from London, adding layer upon layer of detail, some of which will be invisible to the eye. "Justin has given it this epic scale: the costumes, the horses, the grandeur of it all. He was adamant we try and duplicate what we know about that era," says Marshall.

Across the game's life cycle, the ethos has been to immerse the player as fully as possible into the chosen era. Sol had been taken aback at the outcry when they relocated the guillotine from the Concord in Paris to in front of Notre Dame in *Assassin's Creed: Unity*. History meant everything to the game, and Ubisoft was determined this remain true for the film.

Researchers looked into how they painted the walls at the time and how the streets were lit, for historical accuracy. Sammy Sheldon [costume design] tinted clothes the way it was done five hundred years ago.

Nicholson sent Caroline Sol to Christopher Columbus' Tomb, which happens to rest in the city's Byzantine-era Cathedral of Saint Mary of the See. There she spent hours taking photos to frame the distance between the entrance door and the tomb.

In fact, the research discovered a secret doorway hidden within the tomb—another potential escape route provisioned by history. "I looked at the side of the tomb and it wasn't normal; it wasn't fixed," she remembers. "Then I realized there was a closet on the side of the tomb." She immediately got on the phone to Nicholson, and the secret door was built into their replica tomb at Pinewood.

The sheer detail of it all is staggering. Even brief scenes such as a fifteenth-century kitchen created by the prop department in Malta offered an opportunity for incredible historical accuracy. The kitchen doesn't play a big part in the story, the chances are you can only catch a glimpse of the room as Aguilar sprints past, but there are props here that have never been depicted before, items they had discovered in their intensive research. One such example is the small cage that was used to store food so the rats couldn't eat it. The props department found an original from the 1400s and used it to dress the set.

This drive to bring the past to life summed up everything they were trying to achieve. When it came to fifteenth-century Spain, burning with the cruelty of Torquemada's Inquisition, the movie would recount history in close detail. We will feel as if we are walking in Aguilar's footsteps just as Callum does.

CHOREOGRAPHING THE ASSASSINS

STUNT MASTER BEN COOKE, whose impressive resume includes *The Bourne Ultimatum* and the recent, gritty reinvention of James Bond in *Casino Royale*, has the composed view of his craft that seems hardwired into stuntmen. Leaping from tall buildings is all in a day's work. You sense there is nothing a movie could throw at him that would rattle his professional sangfroid.

Predictably, Cooke had a large part to play in the making of *Assassin's Creed*. Alongside the director, he is the man responsible for coordinating and choreographing all the major action sequences in both the past and present. Cooke likens this process to putting together a series of three-dimensional jigsaw puzzles made up of action beats that will be edited together into sequences of the Assassins in full flow.

"I would rather do things in camera," he says. "So instead of using a computer-generated version of the character, I do it for real. You know when it is a real person leaping between buildings. You can feel that weight that only comes from a flesh-and-blood stuntman."

Which, ironically, makes their adaptation something of a throwback to the great Westerns and swashbucklers of the past.

For Kurzel it was all about highlighting the fact that the Assassins are real people, albeit people endowed with extraordinary talent. "They are natural warriors, they are guys who have skills they have mastered throughout their lives and from the lives of those who have come before them," he says. "Each jump had to feel like it was absolutely possible; it just needed skilled people to achieve it. That became a bit of guide. If the jump felt like it was too unbelievable, we got rid of it. It had to be just in-between, in that two metres too long zone, where you think, 'Well, an Olympian might do it.' We want people to marvel at the human conquest of the challenge rather than have it be from the superhero world."

TOP: Stunt master Ben Cooke walks Michael Fassbender through the fight choreography of the bridge scene.
RIGHT: Callum's struggles against the bleeding effect culminate in a fight against Aguilar's memory.

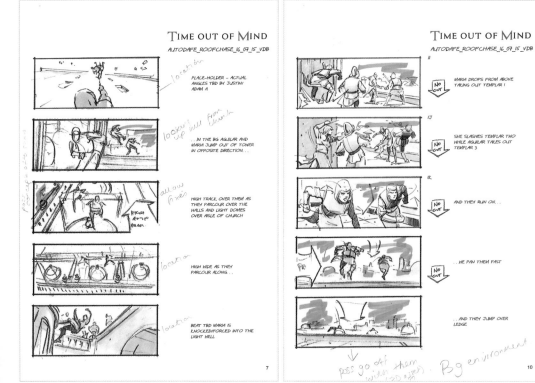

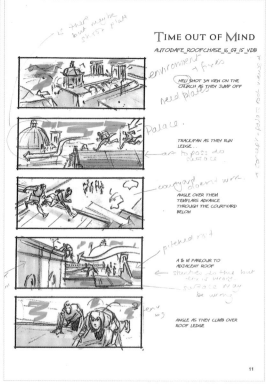

TIME OUT OF MIND

AUTODAFE_ROOFCHASE_16_07_15_VDB

PLACE-HOLDER - ACTUAL ANGLES TBD BY JUSTIN/ ADAM A

.. IN THE BG AGUILAR AND MARIA JUMP OUT OF TOWER IN OPPOSITE DIRECTION...

HIGH TRACK OVER THEM AS THEY PARCOUR OVER THE HALLS AND LIGHT DOMES OVER AISLE OF CHURCH

HIGH HIDE AS THEY PARCOUR ALONG ..

BEAT TBD MARIA IS KNOCKED/FORCED INTO THE LIGHT WELL

7

TIME OUT OF MIND

AUTODAFE_ROOFCHASE_16_07_15_VDB

MARIA DROPS FROM ABOVE TAKING OUT TEMPLAR 1

SHE SLASHES TEMPLAR TWO WHILE AGUILAR TAKES OUT TEMPLAR 3

AND THEY RUN ON...

.. HE PAN THEM PAST

.. AND THEY JUMP OVER LEDGE

10

TIME OUT OF MIND

AUTODAFE_ROOFCHASE_16_07_15_VDB

HELI SHOT 3/4 VIEW ON THE CHURCH AS THEY JUMP OFF

TRACK/PAN AS THEY RUN LEDGE...

ANGLE OVER THEM TEMPLARS ADVANCE THROUGH THE COURTYARD BELOW

A & M PARCOUR TO ADJACENT ROOF

ANGLE AS THEY CLIMB OVER ROOF LEDGE

11

Essentially, the film features three major action sequences aligned to each of Callum's regressions: the carriage chase, the escape from the auto-da-fé, and the raid on the Alhambra. These sequences were then supplemented by additional action cuts completed in the studio, as well as the complex physical requirements of shooting the Animus and a large-scale fight in Abstergo towards the end of the film.

Months of planning were required. First there was an intense rehearsal period where Cooke and his team experimented with different ideas, which they would then record and show to Kurzel for his feedback. On certain occasions Cooke had this team demonstrate them for the director in person. Then, for each location, Cooke needed to figure out the installation of trusses, pulleys, and cranes, the provision of water ballasts, even how many bolts he needed to fix it all in place.

Detailed storyboards and pre-visualization (dubbed "pre-viz," rudimentary computer-animated versions of an action sequence) provided a guide, but Cooke was well aware that once he was on the ground (or on a roof) in a location, everything could change. He had to be skilled to adapt to what each new day would bring. "There may be certain limitations of a location which requires us to lean

OPPOSITE TOP: A stuntman takes a fall off a ledge in the auto-da-fé chase.

OPPOSITE BOTTOM: A selection of storyboards featuring Aguilar and Maria's escape through Seville.

BELOW: Although most of the stunts were performed on location, certain scenes required the controlled setting of the studio.

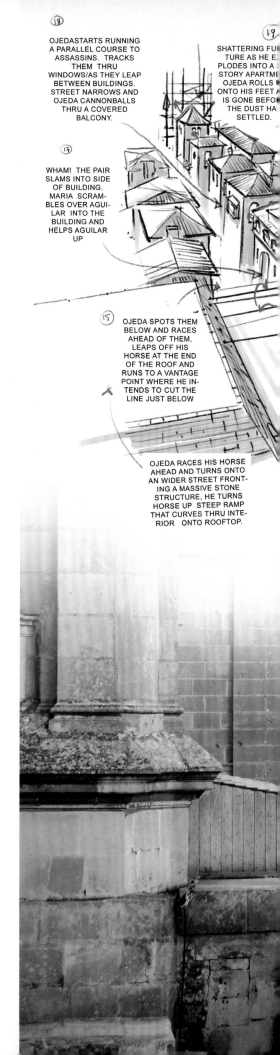

(18) OJEDA STARTS RUNNING A PARALLEL COURSE TO ASSASSINS. TRACKS THEM THRU WINDOWS/AS THEY LEAP BETWEEN BUILDINGS. STREET NARROWS AND OJEDA CANNONBALLS THRU A COVERED BALCONY.

(19) SHATTERING FU[R]-TURE AS HE E[X]-PLODES INTO A [?] STORY APARTME[NT] OJEDA ROLLS ONTO HIS FEET [?] IS GONE BEFO[RE] THE DUST HA[S] SETTLED.

(17) WHAM! THE PAIR SLAMS INTO SIDE OF BUILDING. MARIA SCRAM-BLES OVER AGUI-LAR INTO THE BUILDING AND HELPS AGUILAR UP

(15) OJEDA SPOTS THEM BELOW AND RACES AHEAD OF THEM, LEAPS OFF HIS HORSE AT THE END OF THE ROOF AND RUNS TO A VANTAGE POINT WHERE HE IN-TENDS TO CUT THE LINE JUST BELOW

OJEDA RACES HIS HORSE AHEAD AND TURNS ONTO AN WIDER STREET FRONT-ING A MASSIVE STONE STRUCTURE, HE TURNS HORSE UP STEEP RAMP THAT CURVES THRU INTE-RIOR ONTO ROOFTOP.

on visual effects," he says, "or bring it back to the studio and shoot against green screen. But we would always try and have something in our bag of tricks."

Alongside Fassbender, they had to define a style for Aguilar as an Assassin. Every Assassin has their individual fighting styles and personalized weapons that serve as an extension of their personalities. The lithe Maria (Ariane Labed), for instance, favors a crossbow. The robust Benedicto (Carlos Bardem) prefers a poleaxe.

Aguilar demonstrates a dazzling variety of Assassin techniques: close-quarters fighting (including two extendable blades hidden in his wrist guards), acrobatic leaps, parkour, and even slacklining, all governed by his uncanny ability to read and maneuver through the landscape.

"You have to bring Aguilar the character to life," Cooke says. "How does he move? How does he fight? It's interesting, because within the film he's human. He's real. Yet, he's extraordinary. He's cat-like in his movement. His agility is off the scale. But he still is grounded and human. He's not a superhero."

Indeed, while shooting the more superhuman exploits of Magneto for *X-Men: Apocalypse* in Montreal, Fassbender would spend his downtime in the gym and doing parkour sessions. "To be honest with you," he says. "I could do the basics pretty well, to learn something advanced on that level would be tricky." The priority was being strong enough. At thirty-eight, he needed to be confident in his body, to make sure he didn't turn an ankle or throw a knee—something that would bring the whole production grinding to a halt.

Damian Walters, Fassbender's stunt-double for the majority of the sequences, was impressed by the star's commitment. He watched an actor with almost photographic recall learn entire fight progressions after no more than a couple of rehearsals, freeing them up to improvise more advanced moves. Fassbender would be up on the battlements with them—Aguilar in his natural habitat.

Walters laughs, "At one point we had him running around the edge of a church roof. Like right around, maybe forty feet up. He's on a wire obviously, but running around the edge of the church right on the precipice."

Fassbender found the best way to conquer any fears was to respond counterintuitively. "As an actor you are calling on your imagination," he explains. "When you are doing stuff like that, you try to switch off your imagination. You are trying not to think about the height." There were a couple of moments when he thought he might be developing vertigo, but strangely that was more likely to be on a tower built in the studio than a genuine belfry in Valletta. "I think it has to do with what's beneath your feet," he muses. "It is better if you're standing on something solid."

TOP LEFT: Final result of the jump scene with CGI enhancement.

TOP RIGHT: Notes on the stunts required for escape from the Inquisition.

BOTTOM RIGHT: Aguilar and Maria's jump was filmed using wires and a rigging system for a realistic final result.

(16) AS AGUILAR AND MARIA LAND ON THE TARGETED ROPE, OJEDA CUTS THE ROPE! AGUILAR AND MARIA PLUNGE TOWARD THE GROUND BUT AGUILAR CATCHES HOLD OF THE ROPE, AS MARIA CATCHES HOLD OF HIM! THE TWO SWING BACK TOWARD THE SIDE OF THE STREET THEY WERE TRYING TO ESCAPE!

(10) WITH OJEDA TRYING TO TRACKING THEM FROM THE STREET, A & M DROP TO A COVERED BALCONY AND LEAP FROM ONE TO ANOTHER TO ANOTHER THAT TAKES THEM AROUND A CORNER GIVING THEM ACCESS TO A CHURCH FRONT THAT THEY QUICKLY SCALE AND DISAPPEAR FROM OJEDA'S SIGHT.

(8) WITH A LEAPING ASCENDING WALL RUN HIGH OFF THE PEAK ESCAPE THE COURTYARD BUILDING AND REACH A STEEPLY PITCHED ROOF NEXT DOOR.

(6) WITH A SWARM OF SOLDIERS APPEARING ON THE ROOFS AROUND THEM A&M DROP BELOW THE EXPOSED ROOFLINE TO COURTYARD AVOIDING SOLDIERS POURING INTO THE YARD

(2) THE ASSASSINS MAKE NEARLY IMPOSSIBLE JUMP FROM BUILDING #3 TO A STEEPLY PITCHED, VALLETTA ROOFTOP – THEY LAND ON THE FAR-SIDE OF THE ROOF'S PEAK AND CAREEN DOWN THE TILES TO LAND ON NARROW BUTTRESS SPANNING A DEEP CHASM.

(5) A & M BROAD JUMP FROM BUTTRESS TO BEAM TO BEAM TO SCAFFOLD THAT THEY SWING THRU AND DROP ONTO ANOTHER ROOF.

(12) BUT DOWN BELOW OFF TO THE RIGHT, MARIA SPOTS A SERIES OF LINES CROSSING THE STREET ATTACHED TO THE FACE OF A MASSIVE STONE BUILDING. THE PAIR QUICKLY DROP DOWN TO THE LINES AND START TO CROSS THEM.

ACK LINE QUENCE ERE THE O DODGE TACKS, AP FROM E TO LINE S THEY GHT FOR IR LIVES.

(9) AGUILAR AND MARIA JUMP FROM CHIMNEY TO CHIMNEY ON THE EDGE OF THE STEEP ROOF. A PURSUING SOLDIER QUICKLY FALLS TO THE STREET AMIDST A RAIN OF ROOF TILES THAT EXPLODE AT THE FEET OF OJEDA'S RACING HORSE.

(7) THEY ENGAGE IN A RUNNING BATTLE AS SEVERAL TEMPLARS APPEAR ON THEIR FLOOR. OJEDA RIDES INTO THE COURTYARD AND AGUILAR CATCHES SIGHT OF HIM MOMENTS BEFORE HE AND MARIA RACE THRU THE INTERIOR OF THE BUILDING AND OUT OF A WINDOW OVERLOOKING A NARROW ALLEYWAY SEPARATING THE ADJACENT BUILDINGS

(11) AGUILAR AND MARIA ROOFTOP RUN ENDS WHEN THEY REACH A STREET TOO WIDE TO JUMP! WITH A SWARM OF SOLDIER TO THE LEFT, RIGHT AND BEHIND THEY ARE IN REAL TROUBLE.

(3) SEVERAL TEMPLARS ATTEMPT THE JUMP TO THE PEAKED ROOF BUT LAND SHORT OF THE PEEK AND SLIDE BACKWARDS OFF THE ROOF, ONE CLEARS THE PEAK BUT ROCKETS RIGHT PAST MARIA AND AGUILAR ON THE BUTTRESS.

(4) OJEDA SCREAMS ORDERS TO HIS MEN BELOW. SOLDIERS RACE OFF IN PURSUIT AS OJEDA RACES OFF THE ROOF.

(1) RUNNING A GAUNTLET OF ARROWS, THE PAIR RACE PAST THE CUPOLA TO REAR OF BUILDING.OJEDA BURSTS ONTO THE ROOF WITH SEVERAL TEMPLARS AND LEAP ACROSS THE GAP BETWEEN BUILDING #2 AND #3,

THE REGRESSIONS

DURING CALLUM'S REGRESSIONS, we get a significant glimpse of Aguilar's past when the film unveils Aguilar's initiation ceremony into the Creed.

It takes place in a Moorish fortress used as an Assassin hideout—an actual location discovered an hour north of Almeria (and enhanced in post) where within the mosaic floor the eagle-eyed will be able to discern the symbol of the Assassin Brotherhood. This scene is also our introduction to Maria and Benedicto, who is a mentor figure to the hero.

Encircling Aguilar, all the Assassins chant in unison, and Aguilar grasps a peculiar, ritualistic chopping block. This singular item is the first example of the films' exquisite craftsmanship up close. Like the hilt of sword worn smooth with use, it is stained with the blood of former initiations. Via a hidden mechanism crafted by Tim Wildgoose, the production's armourer, a blade will spring out and slice off the ring finger of an initiate.

"It needed to be more of a ceremonial thing than lying a hand flat on a table," Nicholson explains. "You don't want the character to be flipping the bird at people. So I ended up having a large cylinder with ivory and metal banding."

"Andy thinks how a craftsman would do it," Bourdin says, appreciating Nicholson's dedication to fine detail. "He won't accept something just because it has a nice shape. He wanted the marks of the tools that created the object, to give it credibility."

LEFT: Aguilar's initiation ceremony.

TOP: Concept of the ceremonial block where the Assassins' ring fingers are removed.

THE FIRST REGRESSION—THE SACK OF GRANADA

Seen from an Iberian eagle's perspective—in fact a spider-cam mounted on a cable which swoops down from 80 feet and narrowly misses the heads of the extras—the film's interpretation of the Sack of Granada in 1491 created a vivid battle scene. For our full entrance into the past, Kurzel felt we needed the bristle of a battlefield, and elaborated on historical research with a depiction of a nation at war. Archers, spearman, and Spanish knights clash with Muslim forces outside the city walls.

This required the stunt team to work in concert with visual effects. "We had two armies come together," Cooke says, "and we have people running in. Then we did it again." Visual effects would then overlay one image on top of the other to multiply the number of soldiers, repeating the process until they created an army. But, Cooke explains, they are all real people, not computer generated. Each soldier was armed by Wildgoose's busy armoury department, responsible for conceiving and making the panoply of weapons for the film. If it said in the script that an Assassin cut a man's throat, then Wildgoose came up with a design behind that blade. If a scene required thirty spears with protective rubber tips, he would answer the call.

Having created weapons for everything from *Troy* to *World War Z*, *Assassin's Creed* has been a dream job for the armourer. "I've been a gamer for years," he says. "I've played all the Assassin's Creed games." One of the go-to experts on the game during production, he estimates 20 percent of the film's weapons directly reference the game. "Justin sort of asked me to suggest the weapons that would be best to take from the games and show in the film. And the other 80 percent I designed myself."

Crossing over the battlefield, the story focuses its gaze upon Aguilar and his fellow Assassins attempting to rescue the son of the Emir. Prince Ahmed (Keemal Deen-Ellis) will be plucked from the grasp of the Templars, led by the brutal Ojeda (boxer turned actor Hovik Keuchkerian). And with Maria at the reins, the Assassins attempt to get away with the Prince in a horse-drawn wagon, with the Templars giving determined pursuit. The net result of which will be a carriage chase like no other.

BELOW: Torquemada and Ojeda lead the Spanish soldiers into battle.

OPPOSITE: Granada battle scene concepts.

"I wanted to show how these highly skilled warriors work on moving vehicles," Kurzel says, "how the skills of the Templars and the Assassins were able to navigate that kind of action."

Cooke claims that working with horse-drawn carriages is not so different to shooting a car chase. "You just need the cars to move or, in this case, the carriages and the horses, in a certain continuity."

The chase, like all the major action sequences, works as a story within itself, building suspense, switching perspectives, a throwback to the language of the great Westerns. "Now it's a little more

ABOVE: Artwork of Aguilar and Maria's rescue of Prince Ahmet.

OPPOSITE BOTTOM: Wide shots of the carriage and certain stunts were filmed using real horses. For close-ups, the carriage was pulled by a car.

sophisticated," Cooke says. "Yet we still feel the old-school flavor of it. We've got real stuntmen that aren't on cables doing jumps."

And rather than fake it with a multitude of handheld cameras, Kurzel captured the chase in classical wide shots. "You've got this mishmash of period versus present day methods within the shooting of the movie," Cooke observes. "It's an interesting parallel." Even in the making of the film there is a blend of modern and traditional styles.

THE SECOND REGRESSION—THE AUTO-DA-FÉ

The second of Callum's regressions thrusts us straight into the heart of an auto-da-fé, the Inquisition's terrifying ritual of public penance where the worst offending heretics were famously burned at the stake. Set in Seville, but filmed in Malta, here we find the Assassins—Aguilar, Maria, and Benedicto—captured and shackled to stakes and surrounded by a huge crowd calling for the incineration to begin. In terms of scale alone, it is the film's most ambitious set piece, their most iconic depiction of the Inquisition.

"I found myself staring and thinking, 'Was it really like this?' It was very real," says producer Frank Marshall, awed by both the magnificence of what they built and how it was all at service of such human cruelty. "The pageantry of it. It was incredible."

TOP: Early artwork of the auto-da-fé. When the scene was filmed, the crowd with the effigies would gather on wooden seating.

OPPOSITE: An artist working on the design of King Ferdinand's throne.

INSET: Kurzel reads the script while sitting on the royal stage.

"That was probably the hardest thing to do filming wise," Fassbender winces at the memory of the weeklong shoot. "It was hot in Malta, and along with the flames that arena was kind of like being in a saucepan. Very, very hot. But it was a great sequence."

Since historically the auto-da-fé began its executions in Granada after 1492, the film location was set for Seville, where the Inquisition would strangle their victims before burning them at the stake.

To create Kurzel's version of the auto-da-fé, they purposefully built an entire arena, including the approach and the surrounding rooftops as if it was situated within the city walls. They populated it with a real crowd and had real flames licking at the actors. Kurzel and cinematographer Adam Arkapaw had done wonders with a massive conflagration in *Macbeth*, and he wanted to do something as terrifying here.

"There were a series of grandstands around the central stage," Nicholson describes. "I knew early on it was going to be made out of wood, but it was going to be the gothic woodwork you see in Seville Cathedral where it is very dark. It was a very striking look in the bright sunlight of Malta. Then there was the papal aspect, of people watching the Inquisition, and there was the rabble just there for the sport."

The detail was awe-inspiring. Huge timbers were erected to support awnings made of hand-made Indian fabric to give them a ceremonial feel while shading the crowds. A nearby church clad in scaffolding signals a potential escape route—the kind of three-dimensional thinking that Nicholson had absorbed from the game.

Upon a raised platform granting a perfect viewpoint for the executions were ornate wooden thrones, handcrafted in pitch-black antique mahogany, the tallest of which reached 8 feet high. These were to be occupied by King Ferdinand (Thomas Camilleri), Queen Isabella (Marysia S. Peres), and Torquemada (Javier Gutierrez), the baleful Grand Inquisitor.

To use visual effects to re-create the crowd would have been a betrayal of their philosophy. Instead, they hired 800 extras to create a sequence that rivals the great historical epics of cinema's bygone days. Each extra had their own individual make-up, the work of forty-five makeup artists stationed in a huge tent. Each of the extras was also dressed in an original costume.

The crowd entered in a giant procession bearing banners both papal and pagan. Tina Jones was particularly proud of the effigies mounted on 15-foot poles—thirty voodoo-like gargoyle heads made from bone and wood. As Kurzel reasoned, they would be used to taunt the victims at the stake. "We just took it one step further," says Jones.

Kurzel was excited to depict how evil was investigated and celebrated through costume and through iconography during the Inquisition. "It was all about God and Devil," he points out. "I

ABOVE: The finished set with extras in place.

OPPOSITE BOTTOM LEFT: Ariane Labed talks with Kurzel while chained to a stake.

OPPOSITE BOTTOM RIGHT: The finished set with extras in place.

RIGHT: Sketches of the execution posts and an effigy.

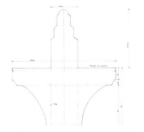

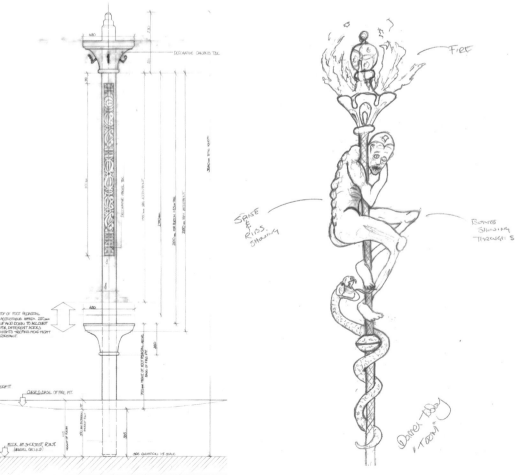

was really inspired by the idea that these characters, the Assassins, have kind of been announced as the children of the Devil."

At the base of a fountain in Abstergo, Jones and her team packed in tiny replicas of the same gargoyle heads. She also points out that in the New Mexico house where Callum lives as a boy, Kurzel thought it would be cool if the camera caught sight of strange, native-themed mobiles made from bits of bone and feather. "We took our reference from the effigies," she says of the film's subtle interweaving of motifs.

The entire sequence is imbued with religious and quasi-religious symbolism. The actual stakes, or execution posts, are intricately carved with a mix of Celtic and Moorish symbols, as well as Nicholson's reference to woodcarvings in Seville's cathedral.

"We had complete artistic license," Jones says, "because in reality if you're going to be burning something it's not going to be so carved and beautiful, but visually it is just so much more exciting."

BELOW: Artwork of the auto-da-fé.

OPPOSITE TOP: The full auto-da-fé set.

FOLLOWING PAGES: Many of the effigies were inspired by pagan imagery and the use of skulls as a symbol for death. The masks for all eight hundred extras were created by hand.

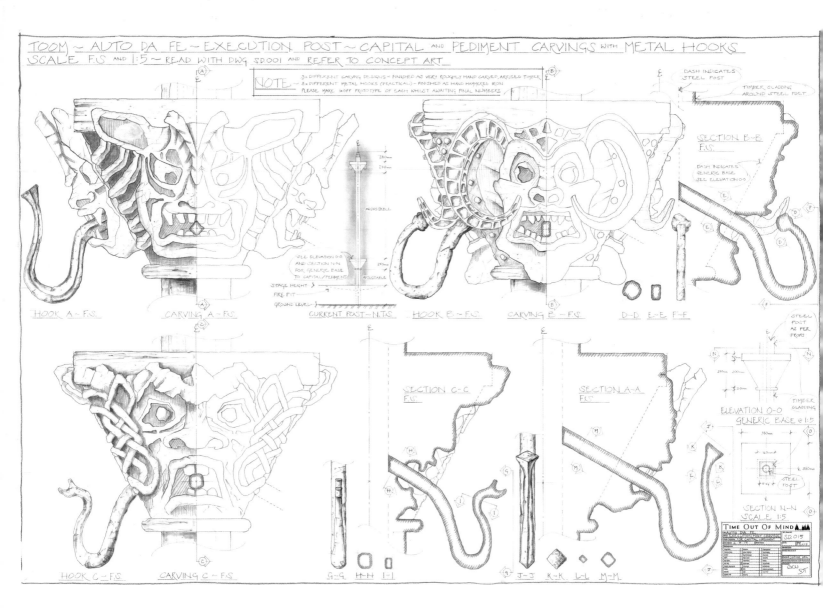

She realized that, with the heroes chained to these posts, they were going to get a lot of camera time.

Fire provided its own concerns for the stunt team. This not only required carefully prescribed safe zones, protective suits, and the precise control of their flames via piped-in gas, but Kurzel also wanted close-ups with dialogue. "Visual effects will be involved," admits Cooke.

Understandably, with flames inches from his head, Aguilar would rather not hang around. A thorny proposition made all the thornier given he and Maria are chained together and must work in unison in the ensuing melee. Just how a manacled Aguilar would liberate himself from the stake was one of the first things Cooke and his team ever discussed. "It was like, okay, how would Houdini get out of this?"

Luckily they had their own Houdini in the unflappable Walters. "My hands were hooked on the pole so they're above my head. And basically I turn 180 degrees to face the pole, then I run up it, unhooking my hands as I back-somersault off the pole. Which was a challenge."

He pauses to reflect on possibly his toughest day on set. "Oh, it was brutal that day. That whole week, actually: It was like 100 degrees, there were hundreds of extras, and it was very dusty and smoky. It looked good, though, really good."

Escaping the pyre is only the beginning of an extraordinary action sequence inspired by the same intense dynamics of the game. Pursued by Ojeda and the Templar soldiers, the Assassins will

TOP: Early designs for the execution posts.

OPPOSITE: Some of the stunt work and practical effects featured in the auto-da-fé scene.

climb up the church scaffolding and out across the rooftops of Seville, jumping off walls, leaping chasms, landing on balconies, and even taking shortcuts *through* buildings, before concluding on the roof of Seville Cathedral (a CGI-enhanced set constructed in Malta). Their parkour skills deliberately matched signature athletics from the game.

"It was about how you can use a city like Seville like a kind of obstacle course," Kurzel says.

When Aguilar crashes through a window into a nobleman's house and begins to career through an endless procession of rooms, Jones was determined nothing about the interior would be predictable. Fleetingly, you can see an arrow maker with piles of feathers and birds in cages.

"So as they ran through there'd be clouds of feathers in the air," Jones explains. "Then they run through a smoking den, a kitchen, a dyeing area with colored walls, all these dressed period rooms. It made it visually really exciting."

Marshall describes it more like ballet than action. "This is a more stylized version of parkour."

While often at the limit of what was physically possible, the action sequences were never about showing off. Cooke and his team responded to the needs of the story, earning the trust of their director. If they planned a spider climb—where two Assassins, back to back with feet planted on opposite walls, shuffle their way upwards—it was because it was the most practical means of getting the characters from A to B.

"Justin wanted that authentic look," Walters says, estimating that 80 percent of the stuntwork in the film takes place in the past. "So you're actually jumping off these buildings. It was very rare

BELOW: Just as in the games, parkour and verticality play major roles in the film's visual style.

OPPOSITE TOP: Maria and Aguilar's handcuffs and chains become the means by which they fight and escape.

OPPOSITE BOTTOM: The professional slackliners filming a scene in which the Assassins run across a banner.

that there were any wires used for safety. We just had the air mats at the bottom, in case you fell off."

While the script stated that Aguilar and Maria remained merely chained at the wrists, Kurzel decided to up the ante. Walter chuckles ruefully, "We're chained by the neck. Our hands and feet were chained. How are you supposed to fight with your hands and feet chained?"

The truth is, it inspired them. As the conjoined characters leap between buildings, Walters decided to have Aguilar do a forward somersault. "It's spectacular," Cooke exclaims. "They're still chained!" When their metal cord is finally severed (by a well-timed axe blow), Aguilar adapts the loose chain as a weapon, whipping it around his foes, or wrapping it around his hand to use as a knuckleduster. All these different elements unite into a continuous state of motion—the heartbeat of the film.

And if, somehow, Walters' skills didn't suffice, they brought in specialists. In a brief almost becalmed moment in the chase, the escaping Assassins come to an alleyway with banners strewn between window ledges, so Cooke figured out they would simply slackline their way across. The stunt-sequence required the expertise of the world champions from Estonia.

Slacklining involves moving along a ratchet strap (the kind of thickened fabric cord used to hold down loads on open trucks), with just enough give to maintain a balance. "These guys can walk on it, somersault on it, run across it," Walters says. "It doesn't look real. The mid part of the body doesn't move, only their arms and legs move. It's the most surreal thing I've ever seen."

THE LEAP OF FAITH

Uppermost of the acrobatics that define the Assassin's Creed universe is the Leap of Faith. This impressive feat finds the Assassin climbing to a vertiginously high location—treetop, tower, minaret, or Notre Dame Cathedral—then diving off, arms outstretched, trusting that he or she will land in a bale of hay (or the equivalent). The exhilarating embodiment of the Assassin's yearning for freedom, the dive is fleetingly transformed into flight.

Given its significance to the franchise, as well as the spectacle it presented, Justin Kurzel felt it was crucial to create a cinematic Leap of Faith. "It is such a great concept, the idea of believing in your instincts, and the voices in your head that say, 'You can do this,'" he explains. "Those voices are actually voices from the past."

The Leap of Faith embodies Callum's journey. At the beginning of the film he just doesn't have it in him to make the jump. Then, as Kurzel says,

"It is about a moment when he realizes that there is an energy in him that makes him feel calm about leaping off a building into nothing and knowing he will survive."

They could have shot against green screen or used a digital double of Michael Fassbender, but stunt master Ben Cooke knew if they did it for real, this would become not only the film's iconic moment, but film-making history. "No one does that anymore," he said to his director. Kurzel didn't take much persuading.

Damian Walters, Fassbender's thirty-three-year-old stunt double, was a man fully prepared to leap from death defying heights for the sake of art. "If you can't do a high fall on this film, you can't do it on any film," he says matter-of-factly. Initially it was planned that the stuntman would jump 30 feet or 40 feet in front of a green screen, but Damien himself suggested that they break the world record and perform the Leap of Faith from 120 feet in the air.

Walters, a big fan of the game, had been planning his own Leap of Faith fan video—from a church tower in his hometown of Derby in the UK—when Cooke called and invited him to join the movie version of Assassin's Creed.

"It's the last part of the second regression," Walters says, pinpointing the fictional location to Seville where Aguilar will leap from the tower of the cathedral. They actually shot it against the beautiful light of Almeria, using four cameras, including one in a helicopter and another on a descender rig, which would follow him down.

Walters built up gradually, executing leaps at increasing heights, mastering the physics of the fall. "We started at 70 feet, then 80 feet, 90 feet, 100 feet, 110, 120. Just built it up and up. To see how high we could get."

Each height differs significantly, with its own "hang-time"—the time Walters had in the air before hitting the 33-foot by 33-foot air bag. "The falling's not a problem," Walters explains, "because you're changing your body position to try and alter how you'll land."

On a standard jump, if you are falling too fast, you try to widen your surface area to slow yourself down. If you're not falling fast enough, you try to lessen your surface area, which speeds you up. It's all a matter of aerodynamics, and, remarkably, a stuntman balances in the air.

"But the problem with the Leap of Faith is the shape he holds all the way down in the video game," Walters says. "And every time you go 10 feet higher, it's a different fall time and it's a different angle. You're doing a calculated guess, but they're still kind of guesses."

Indeed, for his rehearsal at 70 feet, just as Walters left the platform, arms spread like wings, he heard someone on the ground yelling. "I thought they were yelling to me," Walters says. The previous day they canceled a jump as the wind had picked up, threatening to blow away the landing bag, so he was more wary than usual. "It was unfortunate. So I looked down. I saw the bag was fine, but knew I had the angle wrong. So I tucked maybe halfway down. For half the fall I wasn't looking at the bag. I was just waiting, waiting, waiting for that big hit. After that, I said, '*Please* can everybody be quiet?'"

"He said it was like someone had taken a cricket bat to his head," Michael Fassbender says. "So I asked him, 'Do you really have to go for the record?'"

There is something heroically imperturbable about Walters. A few days later he launched himself from 120 feet, and in one take executed the movie's Leap of Faith.

"It was pretty spectacular I must say," Fassbender says with satisfaction.

THE THIRD REGRESSION—THE ALHAMBRA

The third and final regression takes us, finally, to the glory of the Alhambra. However, despite all of Sol's entreaties, the Alhambra's Court of Lions was strictly off limits to filming. So they re-created portions of Spain's most famous buildings from the 2,500 pictures that Sol took of the historical site.

"I used my hand to show the scale and my arm to show size to help Andy as best I could," Sol recalls. "It really helped with the details." Sol's highly specific research included the type of tiles they used on the roof, and the local vegetation. She found a map of Granada dating from 1491 and made copies for the visual effects department to provide eagle-views of the city. When she visited the set in Malta, she was amazed at how accurate it was.

Nicholson admits it was a costly set to build, but you can't shortcut one of the most famous buildings in Europe. "We built the Court of Lions and a portion of the baths," he explains, "which was adapted for the story." There is a hidden compartment located in the wall where the Apple of Eden has been secreted, and they had to provide the grate that provides an escape route for Aguilar.

Echoing Callum's gradual mastery of the Animus, the third regression finds Aguilar and Maria taking control of their mission to protect the Apple of Eden. They throw the court of Torquemada into confusion through the use of smoke bombs.

"The smoke bombs are essential," Cooke says. "That's the heart of what they do as Assassins. So I think that was a really smart choice. Justin really pushed for the smoke bombs sequence as well."

After the wide-open surroundings of the carriage chase and the rooftop vistas of Seville, things become more contained and claustrophobic. Not that this made it any easier to manage. "It's hard to control smoke," Cooke is aware he is stating the obvious. "It's like herding cats. It does whatever it wants to do, and the wind changes."

BELOW: An exact replica of the Court of Lions was constructed for the film.

OPPOSITE TOP LEFT: Maria attacks a Templar soldier after leaping from the courtyard roof.

OPPOSITE TOP RIGHT: Kurzel demonstrates Maria's assassination pose.

OPPOSITE BOTTOM: Ojeda prepares to throw Aguilar forward.

FOLLOWING PAGES: Court of Lions concept.

OPPOSITE TOP: Brutal and ruthlessly efficient, Ojeda proves a challenging adversary to the Assassins.

OPPOSITE BOTTOM: Details of the Alhambra set.

TOP: The exchange for the Apple of Eden.

ABOVE: Smoke bomb.

The bombs, the size of a hand grenade, were designed by Wildgoose to actually work. Made out of glass, you smash them on the floor and out pours smoke. With the help of the practical effects department, they filled the room with a dense fog. Cooke had to choreograph fighting where his stuntmen knew their steps without being able to see where they were in relation to the camera.

"One thing that Michael said early on is that he wanted all his fighting to be really up close and personal," Wildgoose says. "Some of the other Assassins have swords, and Benedicto has a big poleaxe, which is more for distance. But Michael always wanted it to be an intimate sort of fighting."

"It's a very effective way of killing. It's very straightforward. Bang, you're dead, that's it," iterates Walters of Aguilar's throat-cutting techniques. "Obviously if you do that too much in the film, it kind of bores, so you've got to jazz it up a little bit more."

This regression will also include the long-awaited confrontation between Aguilar and that Templar brute Ojeda, which Kurzel delightfully describes as "like a scene out of *Raging Bull*." It was, he says, about fighting in a really intimate way, showing off their skills.

Trailed by Torquemada's men, Aguilar exits through Sol's tunnels beneath the Alhambra to the city walls. Given the lack of access to the actual Alhambra, the perfect proxy was found in one of the oldest forts in Malta, which possessed a labyrinth of corridors inside its walls. The only downside was that the crumbling fortress had lately been used as pig farm. It was a surreal location on the sea, and if you dared to venture down through its maze there was a 100-ton cannon sticking out of the wall.

"It was a Victorian fort built but never used," Nicholson says. "It had been used as a pig farm for fifty or sixty years. When Malta joined the EU, it became illegal for Malta to farm pigs underground."

"The stunt guys were there a lot more than I was," Marshall laughs. "That was when I needed to be back at the hotel to do some paperwork."

THE FINE DETAILS

WHILE THE EMPHASIS HAD BEEN ON SHOOTING on location and making the film as tangible as possible, perfecting the past required digital enhancement. This meant not only the removal of modern intrusions like television cables and satellite dishes, and computer-generated cityscapes for wide shot, but fine tuning the filigree of history.

Unusually, Nicholson stayed on the film into postproduction working with the visual effects team to, as he puts it, maintain the "consistency and authorship" of the film's design.

A slight wrinkle in their quest for authenticity, Malta's capital mostly dated from around seventy years *after* their chosen period. Valletta had been destroyed in the early 1500s by an earthquake and was slowly rebuilt from 1560 onwards. It was also a different part of Europe.

Nicholson explains that, "Malta was a great base from which to begin. It gave you a scale of older buildings, which were fairly unmolested, but we had to come up with this way of overlaying

THESE PAGES: Artwork of historic Seville and the area surrounding the auto-da-fé.

fifteenth-century architecture on top of Valletta architecture." This was a case of adding Moorish facades, and replacing Malta's flat roofs with the pitched style common to Seville. The look of the city, which dominates the sprawling second regression, was their main focus.

Much of Nicholson's postproduction centered on the creation of digital assets: "To turn a balcony in Valletta into a Moorish fifteenth-century Seville balcony, I researched it and designed ten of them to use whenever they were needed." Ultimately, it was about removing the guesswork and maintaining an unprecedented level of historical re-creation.

"As much as possible I wanted to make the past feel as authentic as we could," Kurzel says, "because I think it is a great asset of the game. It is one of the reasons why people are so fascinated by it—it does have an historical integrity, it is not fantasy."

THESE PAGES: Concept art of the Spanish cathedral where Aguilar will perform his Leap of Faith.

CHAPTER 5

COSTUMES AND WEAPONS

LOOKING AND SOUNDING THE PART

IF THE GUIDING LIGHT FOR THE BUILDING of the parallel worlds of *Assassin's Creed* was realism, that counted every bit as much in the costumes and weapons. Justin Kurzel was emphatic on this point: "Right from the beginning, I said that I wanted the materials to feel real, like they come from that period, rather than a kind of cartoon." On every level, he never let them lose track of what was believable. Even the speech patterns of the characters had to be authentic.

Dialect coach Neil Swain, who worked on films with heavy emphasis on dialog such as *The King's Speech* and *Suffragette*, and worked with Michael Fassbender and Marion Cotillard on *Macbeth*, was brought in to finesse the dialogue across the entire cast.

"It makes sense because part of the film takes place in fifteenth-century Spain," Swain says, "and we had Spanish actors, and two French actresses for whom English is not their first language."

Furthermore, any scene in fifteenth-century Spain was to be filmed with the actors speaking with a Spanish accent. Swain says, "It was really important to both Justin and Michael to honor that this is a different world and this game is very much about traveling between different times. But we also did them in English, because it gave a choice to both Justin and to the studio."

Thus any of the actors in the Inquisition sequences had to deliver their lines both in English and Spanish, keeping the same intensity with each. "Poor Javier Gutierrez, who plays Torquemada, has some very big speeches to the crowd," Swain says. "They are very Shakespearean in their scope with a lot of biblical references."

Meanwhile, Fassbender also had to factor in separate vocal styles for Callum and Aguilar. Aguilar would be taciturn, putting more importance in the unspoken communication between the Assassins. Swain likens it to the almost Zen-like communication between Buddhist monks that

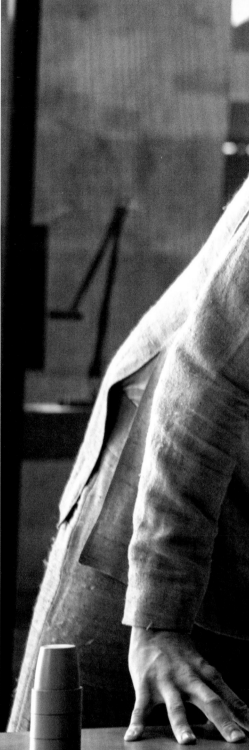

LEFT: Torquemada's costume includes several crosses, both to signify his status as a priest and as a hint to the Templar cross.

ABOVE: Callum's rapport with the other test subjects does not extend to Nathan at first.

comes from a shared belief system. "When we get to Callum, he is very vocal and uses language well," Swain says.

Experienced costume designer Sammy Sheldon, who has worked on films as diverse as *Ant-Man* and *The Imitation Game*, couldn't be more enthusiastic about her work on the project, proving a font of insight on her complex process of research. "I love researching," she says. "You have your period research and you have your character research, which is more emotional. Or more abstract, more elemental. Often I'll go into whether someone is warm or cold. Is there a part of an animal that you can relate to them? What do they eat when they have breakfast?" She worked closely with Kurzel and Andy Nicholson to maintain a harmony between her ideas and the overall design concepts: colors, motifs, and themes all had to be in tune.

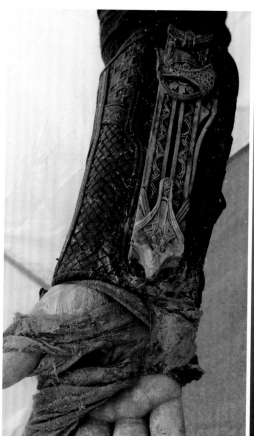

AGUILAR

ONE OF THE LURES of *Assassin's Creed* for Fassbender was the challenge of filling the boots of two leading men, intimately connected via their DNA. They were distinct characters, different people, but the audience would need to sense the connection that stretches across a gulf of more than 500 years.

The dual roles set a similar challenge in terms of costume design—they would need to be distinct, but linked. Confined at Abstergo, Callum's apparel falls somewhere between patient and prisoner. He has been striped down to the bare essentials, and Sheldon thought of a cool, Japanese influence, with a simple two-piece in a fine fabric. "You've got angular lines on them," she points out, "so they're not straight up and down. He is living in a world of Templars. You have to show a bit of both Templars and Assassins in there."

Once Callum has embraced his destiny, Sheldon gave him a coat and hood that deliberately echo the lines of Aguilar's cloak. "It's all asymmetrical," she says. In other words, liberated from the order of the Templars.

When it came to Aguilar and the Assassins in fifteenth-century Spain, Kurzel was very interested in the Moorish influence and how to draw upon a more tribal feel. One of the memorable visual signatures of *Macbeth* had been the pagan mysticism mixed in with the gloomy Catholic grandeur of medieval Scotland. It was a thrilling slant on history.

"I wanted the Assassins to represent free will almost like gypsies and travelers, so their costumes became a collection of influences," Kurzel says. "I also wanted the material to feel worn; I didn't want it to feel contrived in the sense that there were no marks on them. They had to have personality and character. I guess I wasn't so hung up on the costume feeling beautiful."

Giving the Assassins Kurzel's signature face paint gave them both a sense of tribal bonding and re-emphasised the individuality that the Templars see as heretical and pagan. There is something about them that stretches back before religion.

OPPOSITE: Design sketch of Aguilar's costume.

ABOVE: The hidden blade used for up-close shots is fully functional and highly detailed.

"We weren't just doing fifteenth-century Spain," Sheldon says. "We were doing our version of fifteenth-century Spain, influenced by all those beautiful roots of people coming up through Africa and across from Persia."

The Assassins should appear as if they come from somewhere else, but nowhere you could instantly place. They are worldly and nomadic. A "huge spider's web" of influences was, quite literally, sewn into their costumes.

Sheldon would both adhere to history and elaborate upon it, with the Assassin's Creed universe always at the front of her thoughts. Logically, Sheldon started with the game and the bible of information provided by Caroline Sol in mind. She was delighted with what she found. The Assassin aesthetic was always wing-shaped, very flowing and organic, especially compared to the rigid geometries of Templar design.

"That's very easy symbolism to take on board," Sheldon says. "And there's no point in breaking that mold, because we are, after all, making a film based in that world." No matter what era they were dealing with, all of the games held to that eagle-like movement within the look of their Assassins. It embodied not only their physical freedom, but also the fact that they are outlaws, unshackled from any system of rules but their own creed.

THESE PAGES: Dozens of makeup artists give the two armies a realistic appearance.

The game was simply a starting point from which they would explore a tapestry of possibilities. "You can't be too faithful to that," Sheldon says. "You need to be faithful to your script and what your director wants. You just have to gauge it so it becomes its own life."

Again and again, the filmmakers returned to the concept of a living history, that the past will envelop the audience just as it does Callum, helplessly strapped to the Animus. They didn't want anything to feel too familiar, in historical or movie or gaming terms. It had to feel real, not prescribed.

Nevertheless, there was no getting away from the hood. The hood was essential. Through the vast saga of the Assassin's Creed games, the hood that veils the Assassin's face has become as iconic as Batman's cowl.

"I think there is something really attractive and beguiling about hoods," Kurzel reflects. "The coolest part of the whole of Assassin's Creed is the hood."

The hood is the keystone for the entire Assassin iconography; it defines them: furtive, a figure of mystery. As soon as the leading man had been announced in July 2012, fans had one burning question—how cool did Fassbender look in the hood? The answer came with the very first picture released to an expectant public in August 2015, revealing the actor as Aguilar, wrist-blades

ABOVE: Aguilar costume details.

OPPOSITE: Various weapons created by Tim Wildgoose, including an Assassin crossbow, Ojeda's mace, and the guillotine gun from *Assassin's Creed: Unity: Dead Kings.*

unsheathed in a classic pose, his face enshrouded by silvery-grey cloth, into which the symbol of the Assassins has been sewn.

"We probably did about twenty or thirty tests, trying to replicate the hood from all the things that people wanted," says Sheldon. She was juggling not only the expectations of fans, but also of Ubisoft and New Regency, and especially what was needed for the actors. "When you watch the game, they can manipulate that piece of fabric any way they want and it flows in the right way. If he turns his head, it doesn't wrinkle. And that isn't going to work with fabric."

In this particular case, history wasn't overly helpful. Hoods were worn in the fifteenth century, but they tended to taper to a point on top. The hood is one of the aspects that place Assassins slightly outside of time. "But it can't be too flowing," she explains, "because then it looks like Red Riding Hood."

And it needed to move in concert with the actor. If Fassbender turned his head, the cloth must turn with him. But it needed be rigid enough that when he darted about the hood stayed in place.

As Kurzel explains, "We would do little tricks like put wire along the edge, or there would be a skull cap underneath that the hood would be attached to stop it floating up and down. There were a lot of different tricks to make it magically feel like it was sitting on his head."

At the end of this exhaustive, maddening process of trial and error, they arrived almost exactly where they had begun—the game. Clearly, the game's designers had gone through their own agonies of R&D, and the movie hood has a period feel strongly blended with the game's distinctive wing-shaped motif.

Sheldon laughs, "You wouldn't think that hoods would be that complicated, but my goodness they are."

Moreover, every Assassin in the film required their own distinctive hood that tied back into their costume and character. "I had someone embroider the crest on every single Assassin hood," she explains. "It's very subliminal. On Aguilar you can see it, but then it gets watered down for the others; some of them are just a line, but that symbol is there in all of them."

For the costume department, the entire universe of the Assassins orbited Aguilar. He was the focal point of the film. They needed to solve all their costume problems through him, and once solved they could adapt their ideas into the other characters. So, following intensive discussions with Kurzel and Fassbender, and with the script in hand, Sheldon first sat her team down and got them thinking about Aguilar as a character, and the intimate blend between who he is and what he wears.

"We wanted his costume to have a very big Moorish influence," she says. "We put a bit of American Indian into it. Justin was very interested in trying to create protection without using armor."

The design also had to be symbolic. Again Sheldon emphasised wing motifs in the way the beading arches across his chest like an eagle in flight. The beading itself represented bone and metal—earth qualities. "He's from the earth," she says, explaining that there are about 6,000 beads in Aguilar's costume, each one sewn in by hand. "He's centered and honest about where he comes from."

Bone also had an influence on the dark gray color of his costume, to which they added flashes of red. Sheldon had noticed that the game-makers always included flashes of red, like blood, running through their digital Assassins. Look closely at the film version and there are tiny pieces of rubicund coral dotted over Aguilar's halberd.

The body of the costume is made from raw, woven silk, which has a beautiful texture on camera, but was maddeningly prone to distressing. They bound off the edges with hand-woven leather in an America Indian style. Everything had to appear weathered. Aguilar lived in these garbs, killed

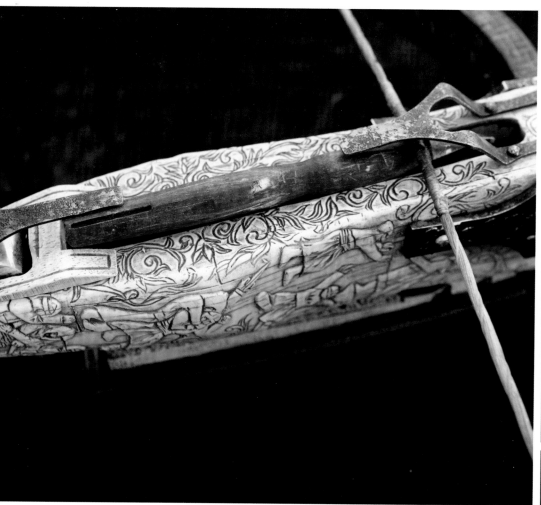

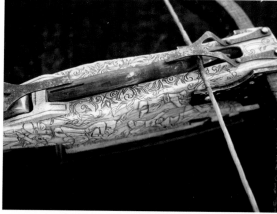

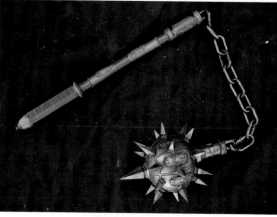

in them. They should feel like a second skin: "It's all layers and layers," says Sheldon. Not just of material, but of character.

For instance, Kurzel wanted to give Aguilar and his fellow Assassins trinkets, small keepsakes, and amulets that signified where they had been. It would be a personal history written into their costumes, which never needed explanation. Sheldon elaborates, "There's little bits of stuff hanging off them like tiny little purses that might contain a seed or a piece of jewelery that means something. There are different kinds of feathers around their belts that are clearly there for a reason."

As for footwear, with the action sequences in mind, Sheldon sought out a boot-maker in Toronto for the parkour soles and strappings inside Aguilar's authentically modeled, fifteenth-century boots.

For Tim Wildgoose, crafting the weaponry for each character followed a similar balancing act of what to take from the game, from history, from the ready supply of ideas from his director, and what was simply practical. He was also intent on imbuing each piece—each Assassin has a personalised collection—with the personality of its owner.

Being an aficionado, Wildgoose always started with the game. "I knew a load of weapons that I thought would lend themselves to either Assassins or Templars. I showed them to Justin and then we'd work out which would be best to assign to different characters. I sort of knew a brief history of the characters. Then I got references for, say, Moorish weapons from the fourteenth century and used those as influence."

Wildgoose then looked at art from the era for the little embellishments. "I always thought the Assassins were more free with their influences. So that's reflected in their weapons."

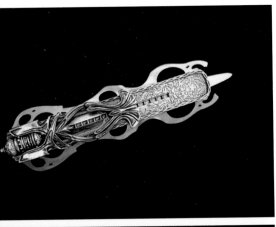

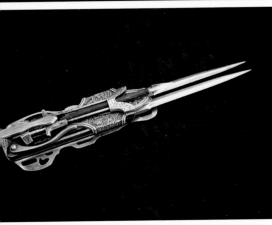

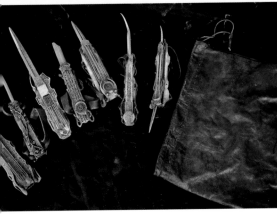

TOP: Benedicto's hidden blade.

MIDDLE: Maria's hidden blade.

BOTTOM: The collection of hidden blades archived in Abstergo's vault.

The process was much like crafting jewelry or holy relics, only they were instruments of death. He worked eagle iconography into Aguilar's wrist-blades along with the Moorish pattern work. "Justin likes to have a lot of the bone and mother of pearl in the Moorish weapons that Aguilar and Maria have. Very fine mother of pearl pieces and fine sculpted bone detail. It's a very Moorish sort of motif."

Something he loved about the game was how players get to pick their own weapons. It was an idea he would invest into the film. Each Assassin favors a unique piece, or as Wildgoose puts it, their "go-to thing." For Aguilar, the up-close killer, the defining weapon is his pair of hidden blades, the most iconic of all the game's catalog of weapons.

"I always saw the wrist-blades as something that an Assassin made themselves, so each one is custom made." Wildgoose likens it to how Jedi Knights ritually construct their own lightsabers in Star Wars. "Each is bespoke to that person. It ties into their costume, and the way they fight."

Where Aguilar has single blades on each wrist, ideal for slicing enemy throats, Maria's wrist-blades are double pronged. "Which is for quick stabbing and then walking away," says the armourer pragmatically.

One of the things Wildgoose has so enjoyed about this assignment is his director's determination to do everything as practically as possible. While this didn't mean actual assassinations, the armorer made sure all the weapons could work in the real world. "It was really tricky," he admits in the case of the wrist-blades. "We based the mechanisms on flick knives and backwards engineered those to make a sort of fifteenth-century version of that."

Theoretically, a small string links the wrist guard to a ring round an Assassin's finger. Extend the finger and the blade flies out. "And ours do exactly that," Wildgoose says.

The actual blades come in a variety of types: sharp, detailed versions for close-ups, blunt metal blades for mid-shots, and very soft rubber blades for fighting or grappling. When it comes to the "actual" slicing, they have cut down versions that will be extended with CGI.

Wildgoose has a department of twenty sculptors, leather workers, metal workers, engineers, and painters. "Between us all, we just build the stuff," he says matter-of-factly. He estimates they must have manufactured somewhere in the region of 3,000 weapons for the entire film. "With Michael we've got ten to fifteen wrist-blades. Then obviously you need to make a version for the stunt doubles." Some of them had moving, clockwork parts, so you could see characters interact with them. The armorer's brief for his team with anything mechanical was "make it look beautiful."

While there are no actual examples of spring-loaded wrist-blades from fifteenth-century Europe, Wildgoose rationalized that flintlock rifles and pistols were beginning to be used, and that Assassin's Creed stalwart Leonardo Da Vinci was certainly devising intricate mechanisms with tiny cogs and gears. So the wrist-blade is *feasible*. However, as they were soon to find, making a blade shoot out is the easiest thing in the world. Making it shoot back in again is really difficult. Weeks were spent figuring out a mechanism able to retract the blade. Wildgoose intently studied videos made by fans who have built their own Assassin's Creed hidden blades, but they didn't bring about satisfying results. Da Vinci–style, they had to figure it out their own. And if they don't actually use it in the movie, it doesn't matter. Wildgoose knows it works.

Finally, he worked the Assassin's Creed crest into Aguilar's wrist-blades, as well as his throwing knives. For the record, he also has one set of smoke bombs hidden on his person.

By the final sequence, with Callum initiated into the Creed, he has his own set of wrist-blades. The modern version comes with that same eagle, with the same dial. But it's all modern materials: carbon fiber and steel as opposed to the fifteenth-century leather and steel.

CALLUM'S SECRET BLADE

For the film's final showdown, a fully initiated Callum and his fellow Assassins infiltrate a Templar gathering at the Freemason's Hall in present-day London. The question was how do you sneak a deadly weapon past airport-tight security? The answer came from armourer Tim Wildgoose, who devised a modern version of an Assassin's wrist-blade that could be assembled from concealed parts.

To create a fully operable prop ready to be slotted together on camera like a deadly 3D puzzle, Wildgoose and his team reverse engineered a complete wrist-blade down into its constituent parts. "Breaking it down into pieces," he explains, "and working out how you could smuggle those pieces into the building."

So the various parts of the hidden blade were hidden in pieces among the Assassins. The face of a wristwatch hides the dial that retracts the blade. The long, thin spring pin was concealed inside a pen. There's a piece inside a mobile phone case, a piece hidden in a shoe, one disguised as a belt buckle, one that is the pendant of a necklace, and the large back piece is secreted inside the spine of a book. "It's a really awkward piece to try and hide as it's long and rectangular," Wildgoose says, "and it just lent itself very well to being in the spine of a book. And because we were on Freemason soil, and we've got all these Templar priests and logos everywhere, we basically made a Templar Bible and this piece is in the spine."

All of the separate pieces, as Wildgoose puts it, reflect the Assassin aesthetic: "For instance, the watch has an Assassin logo and the hands make each form into an "A" at the end.

In the film, each of the team of modern Assassins sneaks into the Templar ceremony carrying a separate piece. As they waft past one another, the wrist-blade is inconspicuously passed on with the next piece of the puzzle added. "You see them putting all the pieces together," says Wildgoose. "And that final finished piece is handed to Callum."

By strapping it to his wrist, Callum demonstrates that he is ready to answer his calling.

THE OTHER ASSASSINS

AS WELL AS HELPING SHAPE HIS OWN CHARACTER, Fassbender's role as producer meant he had an input into all the key choices on the film, including casting. There were big names in the mix to play Maria, the female Assassin as formidably agile and deadly as her companion. But through Fassbender's dedication to finding the right chemistry, they would take another leap of faith with the relatively little-known indie actress Ariane Labed, known for art house science-fiction drama *The Lobster*.

Born in Greece to French parents (she is Greek speaking), Labed threw herself into the training with the same fervor as her co-star, dedicating hours in the gym to becoming proficient in parkour and using a crossbow or blade as if born to it (as Maria is). With her background in dancing, Labed was adept with her stunt-team's tricky choreographies.

"Maria is a very straightforward character in many respects," Kurzel says. "She believes in the Creed; she doesn't need to prove anything. I just thought that Ariane is such an interesting and beautiful-looking person, and there is something that is mysterious about her as well."

All three principal Assassins work from the same basic costume. For example, each of their cloaks divides into four at the waist with each segment weighted so that the skirts splay out beautifully as they move and spin. Yet they also embody the multicultural variety of both the game and Inquisition-era Spain. Maria displays North African Berber influences, and her hood is a blue-gray woven fabric shaped into a wing and fine enough to flutter as she moves.

TOP: Maria's Berber-inspired costume stands out from the simplicity of the Granada villagers' clothing.

OPPOSITE: Maria costume sketch.

The fact she was a woman made her costume slightly more challenging for Sheldon. "You're making something look armoured without loosing that femininity, which is difficult." Maria's chest piece was artfully wrought from gold silk, with layers of water beads and tiger-eyes so that it resembles a tribal necklace—another subtle injection of the pagan.

Wildgoose gave her a bone crossbow as well as a parrying shield. "It's like a glove with a five-pointed bladed star coming off the end of it. When someone comes at you with a sword, you trap it in between two of the blades and then twist it to snap the blade."

THIS PAGE: Maria costume details.

OPPOSITE TOP: Benedicto's clothing features trophies and artifacts that the Assassin keeps on his belt.

OPPOSITE BOTTOM: Callum confronts Joseph.

Played by veteran Spanish actor Carlos Bardem—brother of Javier—Benedicto, Aguilar's stocky mentor, hails from Seville. Hence his weapons, particularly the hefty poleaxe he favors, have a curly, leafy sort Spanish metalwork compared with Aguilar's bony Moorish equipment. "There is a distinct difference between where the Assassin is from and what their weapons are," Wildgoose notes.

While it is a Templar facility, Callum isn't the only Assassin to be found at Abstergo. One of these is Joseph, Callum's father, played by Irish actor Brendan Gleeson. Joseph has been subjected to repeated sessions in the Animus, until the Templars realized he wasn't in possession of the necessary DNA. It was Callum's mother who carried Aguilar's lineage.

Callum and Joseph, dressed in similar two-piece patient uniforms, will share an intense confrontation. "Your blood doesn't belong to you," his father tells him, desperate to protect both his son and the artifact. A prisoner in every way to Abstergo, Joseph has lost hope. Callum restores that hope.

THE TEMPLARS

MARION COTILLARD'S SOFIA might be linked by blood to the Templar order, but her affiliation remains elusive, which presented Sheldon with a challenge. "You don't know where she lies as you go through. The first time Callum sees her, we wanted her to have a clinical look." Sofia wears a top with a square neck, beautifully designed but with a Templar shape within it. "It also looks a little bit like a clinical tunic," Sheldon notes. "Later on she's got this little dress as a nod to her being more feminine—a slightly Audrey Hepburn–esque look."

Yet everything she wears is gray, black, and white. Sheldon doesn't want us to notice what she wears, because she is all about her work. "It's not like she doesn't care," she adds. "Her choices are beautiful but always functional. She is quite ambiguous."

While more evidently a villain, Alan Rikkin is also something of an enigma. He believes that humanity cannot live alone and that the elite need to run the world. Not as a dictatorship, but as wise people. He's an elitist, and he thinks the elite should run the world.

The head of Abstergo is played by British master Jeremy Irons, an actor who brings with him a fine history of movie villainy, including an Oscar-winning Count Von Bulow from *Reversal of Fortune*, *The Lion King*, and, in keeping with the game, Rodrigo Borgia from the television series *The Borgias*.

"I could see Jeremy and Marion together, as father and daughter," Kurzel says. "Rikkin has some very strong, ideological speeches made throughout the film and I thought that he would bring a clarity and authority to those speeches."

For Sheldon, it was important to bear in mind Rikkin was a gentleman. "He wears really expensive clothes. But you want him to feel as if he's making a choice to look more comfortable than he should because he's trying to manipulate the situation."

Rikkin's dress fluctuates with his agenda: We see him in a suit, in a sweater and necktie, and in Japanese-inspired clothing—all depending on the situation. "It's quite tricky to map those choices," Sheldon says. "It's quite psychological, everything that's going on. And you also don't want it to be distracting. He was tricky; you don't want him to appear as if he's overdressed."

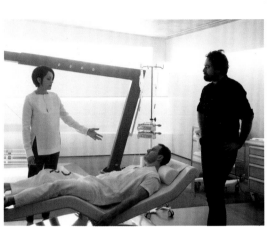

OPPOSITE: Marion Cotillard on the set of Alan Rikkin's office.

ABOVE: Sofia's white top and square collar mimic the clean, clinical appearance of the recovery room.

BELOW: From the robes of a Templar Grandmaster to the suit that he wears for his interview in London, Alan Rikkin favors dark colors and uncomplicated designs.

Alan Rikkin
Chief Executive Officer

arikkin@abstergo.com

ABSTERGO INDUSTRIES MADRID, SPAIN

+34 699 731 721   Abstergo.com   +1 646-845-9162

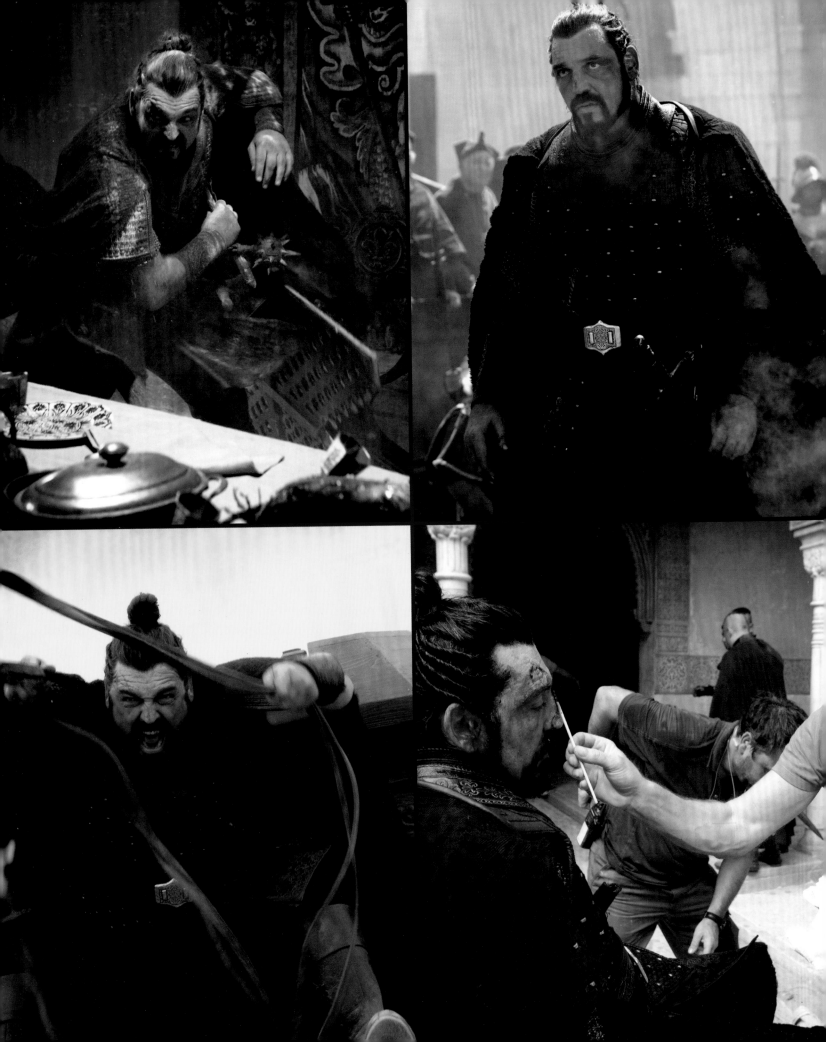

Chief of the Templar forces in the hotbed of the Inquisition is Hovik Keuchkerian's formidable Ojeda. A match for Aguilar, he needed to exude strength and drama. There is something almost gothic about him.

"We wove all his leather, because I wanted to have a slight Samurai feeling to him," Sheldon says, noting that she also had to allow for the number of stunts involved. Everything plays on a square with Ojeda, the right angles reflecting the Templar visual style. It is only his collars and belt, carved with a Spanish influence, which reveal a flourish.

"I always thought his weapons were going to be grotesque," Wildgoose says. "I mean, he's basically a brute, so he has this mace on the end of a chain: a really, horribly spiky thing." They actually made a real one, but it was too heavy even for the stuntmen.

Of particular interest, however, is his sword. With a fine touch of historical nuance, the pommel features a carved ivory head of the first Grand Master of the Knights Templar, Hugues de Payens. It's not something that is referenced in the script, just another sublime detail provided by the creative departments.

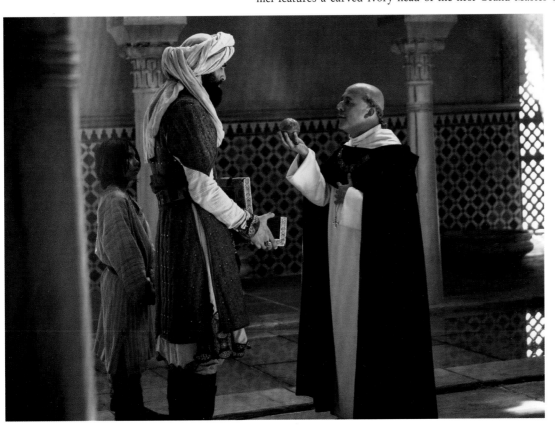

"We found a painting of him and did a 3D sculpture from that," Wildgoose explains. "The idea was with him being the most loyal Templar, he would have Hugues de Payens on his sword."

Correspondingly, there were also many paintings of Torquemada to refer to, Sheldon confirms. "He was a monk. And you can't really step away from that. It's better to be honest about those things, I think. We gave him a bit of jewelery that would signify that he was heightened, and he had his little Templar cross."

In general, Wildgoose kept the difference between the "V" of the Assassin and the square of the Templar throughout all of his weapons. "The Templar was to be hard, straight-edged," he says. "A lot of castellation in the design." The contemporary Templar weapons all bear the same design elements as the fifteenth-century weapons but made with modern materials. This is another good example of the hold the past keeps on the present: Rather than automatic weapons the guards of Abstergo utilize classical crossbows and blades.

Together with his director, Wildgoose decided the Templar tradition still held true in the modern day. "They are very traditionalistic," he says. "They still wear the Templar crosses. The idea is that their fighting styles and their martial arts have continued on. And that carries on with their weapons. It's almost ceremonial in a sense."

Indeed, for a late ceremonial scene, Sheldon dressed her Templars in hooded cloaks like "columns of black." The idea was that their costumes would link directly back to the stark monk-like dress of Torquemada. "The thinking was always, how can we pull it forward?"

OPPOSITE: Ojeda's costume features detailed leather tooling and subtle patterns in the fabric.

ABOVE: The square, rigid angles of Torquemada's costume match the Templar visual language.

CHAPTER 6

THE ARTIFACT

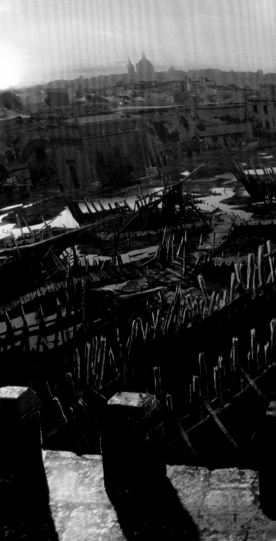

DISCOVERING CHRISTOPHER COLUMBUS

A BELOVED FEATURE OF THE GAME is the opportunity for players to interact with significant figures from history. Not simply famous figures, but leaders, revolutionaries, and artists, those few who can lay claim, for good or ill, to having changed mankind. Some prove to be Assassins, while others are Templars. The aforementioned Leonardo da Vinci, Charles Darwin, George Washington, Karl Marx, even Queen Victoria and Napoleon Bonaparte, have all crossed paths with Assassin's Creed. So it made total sense that the filmmakers introduce their own heavyweight cameos.

Given their story was partly set in the Spain of 1491, this gave them Torquemada and the Spanish royals. But it also offered the chance to come face to face with Christopher Columbus.

"There are certain sort of figures that fit the opposing ideologies," Kurzel says. "You can associate Torquemada with the Templars, and it was much easier to associate Columbus with Assassins. An explorer who found the New World had the personality traits you would associate with free will."

Moreover, they reasoned that as Aguilar battled to save the Apple of Eden, Columbus would be busily preparing for his fateful voyage to find an alternative route to the Indies, and accidentally discover the New World in the process. So Nicholson thought their version of the intrepid explorer would be found in a Spanish shipyard, shot in an alternative Maltese fort that would be enhanced with CGI.

Nicholson did a lot of concept art for their shipyard and is clearly pleased with the outcome—a graveyard of old vessels. "Ships were launched on the spring tide, so the shipyards tended to be built in muddy estuaries," he explains. "I really liked the idea of having this muddy place where there are carcasses of boats that have been stripped for other boats, all these skeletal forms. And the water would be silted up with mud. It was just a nice image."

Pivotally, Aguilar hands over the Apple to Columbus for safekeeping, a scene shot in a small cabin set built in Pinewood, and if you strain your eyes, you can spot the Assassin's Creed crest carved into the walls. The final moments of the third regression—indeed, the final moments in the past—will disclose the present day whereabouts of the Apple to Rikkin and Sofia.

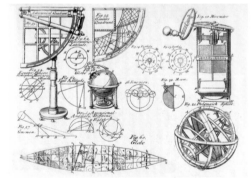

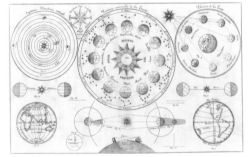

ABOVE: Various navigational charts created for Columbus' ship.

OPPOSITE TOP LEFT AND TOP: Set decorations and concept art of Columbus' ship.

ABOVE LEFT AND RIGHT: Concepts for Columbus' tombstone.

INSIDE THE APPLE

ONE OF A SERIES OF PIECES OF EDEN, the Apple is a powerful item that will allow the Templars to achieve their ends. This, of course, is an oversimplification of its function in a universe as dazzlingly arcane as *Assassin's Creed*, and a director determined that every constituent part of his film has a truth to it no matter how far-fetched. The Apple is not only the object of the Templars' quest, it is fundamental to the film's themes of DNA memory and the root cause of violence.

While the Apple is the goal of the Templars, it isn't the main point of the story. The artifact is something that needs to be protected, but isn't the heart of the movie. Through the search for the artifact, they tell the human story of Callum.

Still, the Apple warranted an extraordinary amount of conceptual thinking. According to the game, the Pieces of Eden were once used by the First Civilization to control mankind, and the Apple is the very same forbidden fruit discovered by Adam and Eve (the very first Assassins). Other Pieces include the Shroud that gave Christ his powers, a sword used by King Arthur, and Crystal Skulls scattered through Central and South America. Such mythology, of course, falls outside of the immediate concerns of the film, where the Apple is closer to a scientific instrument.

If the Templars find this artifact, they can then use it as a kind of DNA road map to locate free will within humans and then supress it.

As Kurzel says, "Templars throughout history have tried to control humankind through religion, through politics, through capitalism, and now they've found a way to control humanity through science."

Marion Cotillard likes to assign a more symbolic purpose to the sought-after item. "It is the symbol of separation. It is the symbol of revolution. And, I would add, it is also the symbol of free will."

Whatever its purpose, it lies secreted beneath many layers of protection. Let us work our way to the center.

ABOVE: Torquemada finally discovers the Apple of Eden.

RIGHT: Alan Rikkin activates the Apple.

THE BOX

Concealed in a hidden compartment within the walls of the Alhambra, the Apple itself is stored in a specially designed chest. Created by Tina Jones' prop department, they knew it had to be a thing of beauty in keeping with its surroundings.

Jones reveals that this box is based on genuine, ornately carved Byzantium designs that would originally have been wooden with ivory layered on the outside. "We re-created carved ivory with bits that were flaking off," she says. "That was a really nice reference, because it just looked like it had been handled a lot." This kind of weathered quality appealed to Kurzel and the overall appearance of the film.

Inside the box, they made a scoop to hold the Apple rather than have it sitting on a bed of fabric like in a jewelery box. That, she rationalized, would long since have disintegrated. "Then we inlaid the crest into it," she says. "It's a beautiful prop, really lovely."

Of course, the box couldn't be made from real ivory; it is a sculpted resin made to look like ivory that is then cast so they can create repeated versions of the box, something true of all the principal props. Jones does a quick tally: "We always do our 'hero' one and then we did a rehearsal one and then we'd have a replacement 'hero' one in case it got stolen or damaged."

TOP: The Emir retrieves the box from its hidden compartment in the wall.

RIGHT: Concepts of the box featured cracks and weathering to give the ivory an ancient, storied appearance.

Within the box, the Apple is still contained within a small leather pouch, for which Jones added an extra bead to the pull-string and engraved it with the Assassin's crest. "It's that little extra something you like to give to a director," she says. "You can show him on the day and he's really excited about it. I think our job is to sort of provide what he wants plus a bit more."

THE APPLE

When we finally glimpse the Apple, what we see is the stone protective casing. As Nicholson observes, it should feel very old, very protected, and very established.

"Justin wanted something more rooted, something a bit more gruesome," Azaïzia says. "Maybe the Apple's been broken and something inside could be like nanotech and moving and evolving."

Like the Animus, the Apple has gone through its own design evolution. Jones can clearly remember their first show-and-tell with the director. They were about three weeks from shooting, and initially Jones and her team had given the Apple the texture of carved volcanic rock. "It's difficult, I think, for a director," Jones says, "because there's so many things that they have to consider. We sort of put him on the spot a bit. And he really needed to think about it."

According to Jones, Kurzel came back with a "lovely idea" of how the Apple would be almost like amber so that you could hold it up to the light. It glows and pulses from deep within. She admits there was a lot of back and forth, with Kurzel already in Malta and Jones sending out samples. "We tried all sorts of different methods. Eventually we solved it and used a dark, ambery resin with screwed up bits of chocolate paper inside to give it sort of glow."

Noticeably, the outer skin of the Apple has been inscribed with swirling, intersecting lines that suggest star charts or runes, alluding to the properties that lie at its center.

The secrets within the Apple, what is pulsing at its core, fell to Virginie Bourdin to fathom. "I took a lot of care with Andy to have a logic within the machine inside the Apple," she says. "So it makes sense. And we can create a story out of it."

As Nicholson reports, "When you get to the final scene, and Rikkin breaks it open to reveal the metal object within, it has a mechanical, molecular movement, which will then start to project the map of DNA. This guide to the genetic code, which isolates different facets."

The film concludes in the actual Freemason's Hall in London's Covent Garden, which has been a Masonic meeting place since 1775. The Masons have long associations with the Templars, but Frank Marshall says they loved having them there. The current art-deco temple was constructed between 1927 and 1933, and within its halls the drama will reach its tumultuous conclusion. Rikkin unveils to the Templar elders that he finally has the Apple, but the Assassins interrupt his moment of glory. But not before he cracks open the Apple . . .

Where Nicholson suggests the inner workings of the device are better left "opaque," Bourdin has gone some way to conceptualizing a living system within the artifact. The core of the Apple, she explains, is encased in the rare metal Gallium. Gallium cannot be found in nature. It has to be extracted. It also tends not to have an orange glow, but Bourdin says, "You can get too literal." One significant property of Gallium is that it melts at a relatively low temperature (85.6 °F), which is far below the average human body temperature (98.6 °F). When a human opens the outer casing, the heat from their body melts its Gallium heart and triggers the Apple.

TOP LEFT: Concept of the Apple's bag.

ABOVE: Various Apple designs.

OPPOSITE: Concept of the Apple's casing melting.

Activated, it works in reverse to the Animus, which takes organic matter and turns it into digital data. As it melts, the Apple turns digital data into organic matter—it literally creates life.

The Apple then displays an intricate holographic projection. Given that it was a literal map of life, Bourdin decided the images projected from the Apple should be a vision of living DNA interacting with proteins.

"What you are going to see is a map of all the connections that are responsible for proteins creating certain behaviors," she says. Stylistically, the visual effect is a mix of ancient Polynesian star charts with the structure of a protein molecule. "If you unroll a strand of DNA," Bourdin explains, "and just show one part of it, that is what is inside the Apple."

The whole design and functionality of the Apple is something that Bourdin worked on into postproduction, refining the look and otherworldly nature of the item. It is the film's key link to the game's mythology, a minute taste of what the First Civilization might be, and what they might be capable of doing.

Much of this work has been about creating a platform for what might be depicted in future Assassin's Creed films. While in this first film, it is has a clear function involving DNA, the Apple could be used as something far more destructive.

THE FUTURE OF THE PAST

WHAT IS FOR CERTAIN is that the door has been left wide open for extending this universe even further. There are the other Pieces of Eden, yet to be found. And the battle between Assassins and Templars is far from done. There is the potential for all kinds of different stories and settings. After all, the whole of history is open to them.

There are new games and advancements of the mythology constantly in development that will fold in the events and designs of the movie. Assassin's Creed's Brand Content Director Aymar Azaïzia explains that the brand has fully embraced the film's elaborate evolution of the Animus, even building up to it in books by introducing more physical versions of the machine. From the film they have extrapolated that the Templars have numerous similar facilities across the world (a map in Alan Rikkin's office points out their whereabouts). And the Assassins have managed to get their hands on the technology. "They are working on their own version," he says, "but it's still a bit old school."

Kurzel states that there is no denying the potential in this material. "Assassin's Creed goes beyond a one-dimensional entertaining game," he says. "It has something behind it that people tune into psychologically, something that is really relevant and interesting."

LEFT: By refusing to kill his father, Callum steps onto his own path.

TOP: Ultimately Callum must decide his own fate.

SEARCHING FOR MEANING

AS AGUILAR HANDS OVER THE APPLE to Columbus, something significant occurs. Viewed through the Animus, blending Callum into the image, it is as if Aguilar is handing over the artifact to his descendant. Aguilar says, "Take it and hide it" to Columbus, but actually he is saying it to Callum.

It is in this moment Callum realizes his destiny.

When UMP set out on their journey to bring Assassin's Creed to the screen, they were determined to break the spell of video game adaptations and make something unique. They wanted their film to mean something. In fact, it means many things.

"For me," Nicholson says, "part of the flaw we have as a race is that we don't live very long. Whatever happened last year no one cares about anymore. If we ever lived to be 200 or 300 years old and remembered everything, the world would be a very different place. That is part of what the regression is for a character. I like that part of it, acknowledging the past, acknowledging what things were within that."

"I would say that it was about the origin of violence," Cotillard says. "Sofia is searching for a cure for violence, but what she should be looking for is reconciliation between human beings."

From the very first conversation Kurzel and Fassbender had about Assassin's Creed, this so-called videogame adaptation has been the catalyst for some profound thinking on the director's behalf.

"To me the film is about the idea that what has come before us in our history tells us everything about who we are and who we are going to be," he says. "That our fate is not wrapped up in our death."

He explains that we have a responsibility to live a life as full as we can, because that life can be passed over and inherited by someone else. When you die all the experiences and effort and knowledge, all the loves and disappointments, don't die with you, they live forever, passed on through your children.

Kurzel elaborates. "This film is an origin story about a man who discovers who he is through his past, and understands that he is part of the Creed. And I am part of a Creed—when you look back to your parents and grandparents and even further, you come from a bloodline and that blood exists within you. That your life could be centuries old really is a deeply moving idea."

Furthermore, the eternal battle between the Assassins and the Templars has the universal theme of the human condition: We all need some sort of control because if we don't have it, we don't advance as a society. At the same time, we pay a price for that freedom. History is a dance between the two philosophies. What is the cost of free will? What kind of sacrifice will free will require?

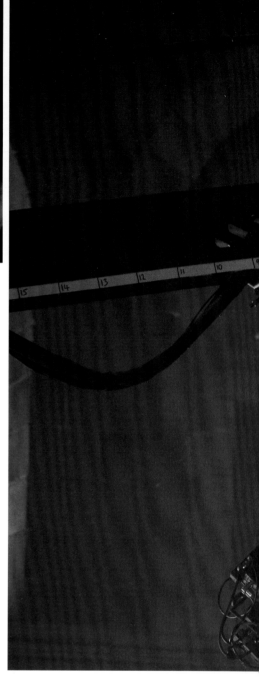

TOP LEFT: Christopher Columbus takes the secret of the Apple to his grave.

ABOVE: Michael Fassbender preparing to film the Leap of Faith in the Animus.

FOLLOWING PAGES: Concept of full synchronization with the Animus.

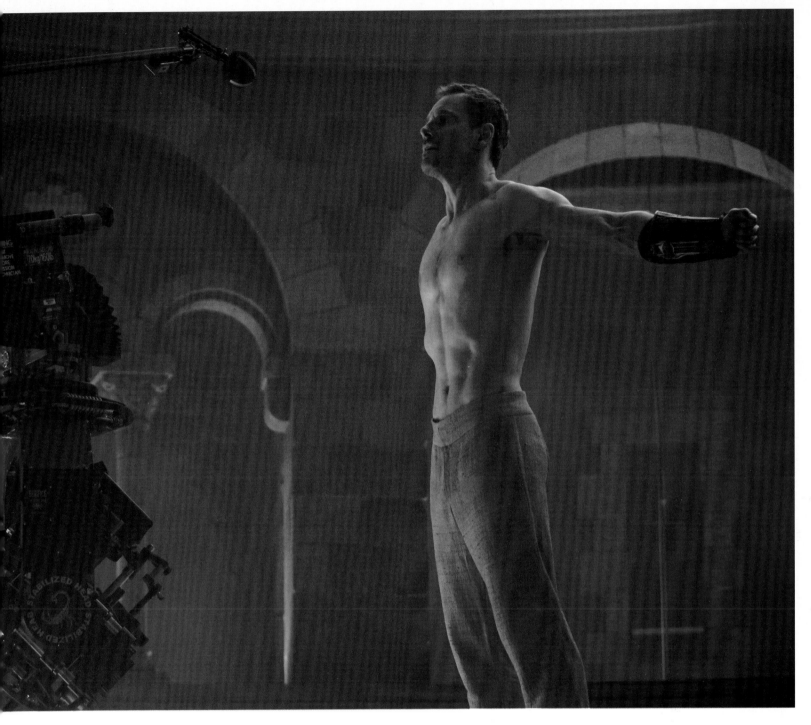

You could say that this film, so immersed in the past, is really about grasping the future. As Maria says at one point in the film, "Today is as important as what we leave behind."

In other words, live in the now. Seize the day.

The Animus itself configures as a metaphor on many levels—of gaming: where Callum is linked by a "controller" to Aguilar; of cinema: the idea of watching and experiencing what another character goes through; of the entire universe: where we battle to control our lives and not have them controlled.

Ultimately, through all the performances, the stunning production design, special effects, costumes, stuntwork, and cinematography, all the immense effort that has gone into *Assassin's Creed*, it is also about the audiences' imagination. The film offers an answer to what life was like 500 years ago. It gives a taste of what it would be like to freerun across rooftops or leap from a cathedral 120 feet off the ground. And, just for a moment, it will feel like flying.

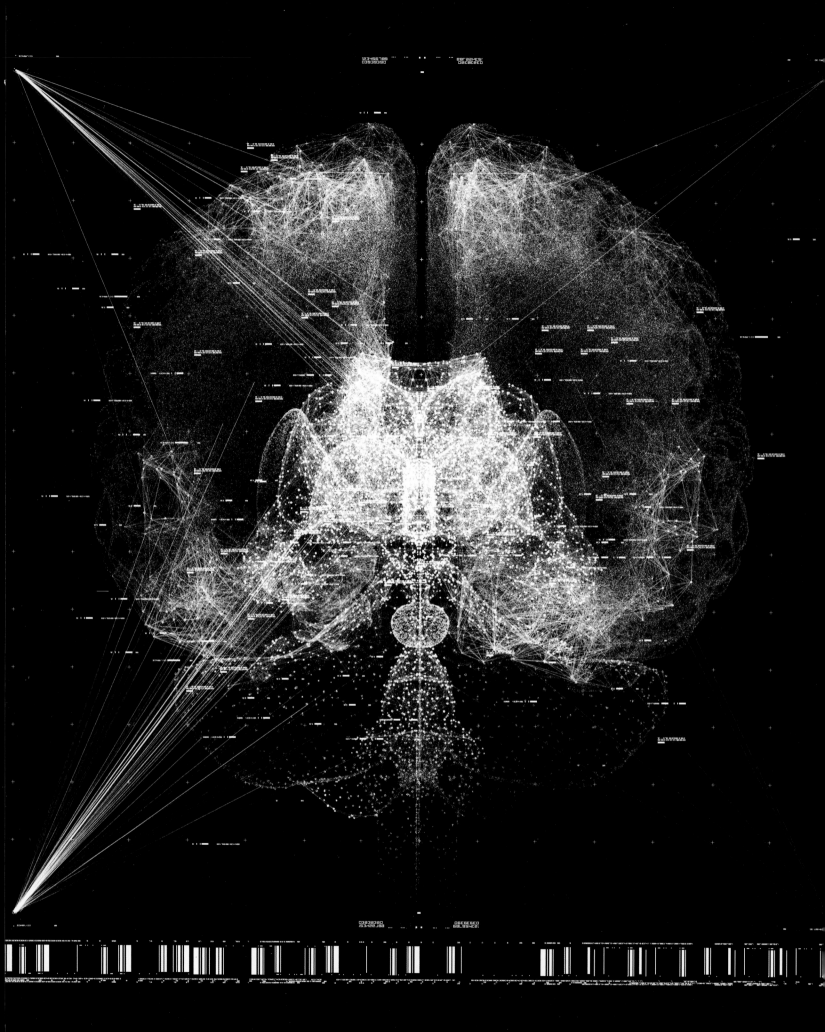

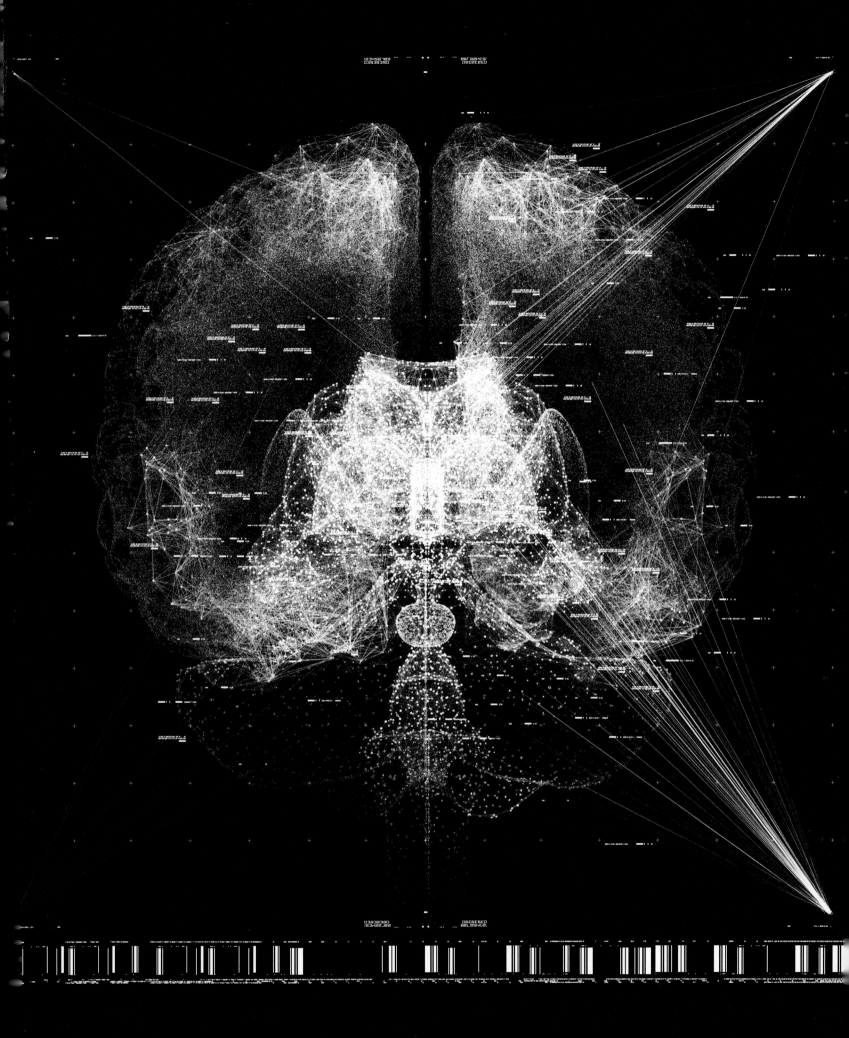

TITAN
BOOKS

144 Southwark Street
London SE1 0UP
www.titanbooks.com

Find us on Facebook: www.facebook.com/TitanBooks

Follow us on Twitter: @titanbooks

Published in the UK and Ireland, Australia and New Zealand by Titan Books,
London, in 2016. All rights reserved.

A CIP catalogue record for this title is available from the British Library.

ISBN: 9781785654633

Published by arrangement with Insight Editions, PO Box 3088, San Rafael, CA
94912, USA. www.insighteditions.com
PUBLISHER: Raoul Goff

ART DIRECTOR: Chrissy Kwasnik

DESIGNER: Jon Glick

EXECUTIVE EDITOR: Vanessa Lopez

ASSOCIATE EDITOR: Katie DeSandro

PRODUCTION EDITOR: Rachel Anderson

PRODUCTION MANAGER: Carol Rough

PRODUCTION COORDINATOR: Leeana Diaz

PRODUCTION ASSISTANT: Sylvester Vang

UNIT PHOTOGRAPHY by Kerry Brown

ARTIST CREDITS:
Sevendalino Khay (8–9, 100–101, 104–105, 112–113, 116–117, 120–121),
Arnaud Valette (95, 98–99), Tony Nguyen (62–63, 68–69), Philippe Gaulier
(97, 122–123), Jonathan Whicher (23, 62–63, 64–65, 66 bottom, 68, 70 top and
middle, 121, 152–153), Levente Petterffy (67), Stephane Levallois (61 left, 66
top, 68 right), Virginie Bourdin (23, 60 right, 62–63, 64 bottom, 65 bottom, 66
top, 152–153), Andrey Riabovichev (66 bottom), Kamen Anev (151), Florian
de Gesincourt (13), Jonathan Opgenhaffen (20–21, 70 top and middle, 71 top),
Gerald Blaise (40 bottom right), Graham Page (71 bottom), Ash Thorp and
Ryan Cashman (4–5, 32–33, 62–63, 79 right middle and bottom, 158–159),
Max Berman (106–107), Gregory Fangueaux (38–39, 40 top, 42–43 middle and
bottom, 59 bottom), Matt Wynnes (42–43, 44 bottom right, 47 bottom), Tim
Wildgoose Company (54–55), Marc Holmes (62–63), Kurt Van der Basch (93
top, 108 insert), Gerard Dunleavy (152–153), Andy Nicholson (35, 38 bottom, 60
left, 101, 102 top, 105 top).

ADDITIONAL ARTISTS: Gerard Dunleavy, Olivier Pron, and Darren Tubby.

ROOTS of PEACE   REPLANTED PAPER

Insight Editions, in association with Roots of Peace, will plant two trees for each
tree used in the manufacturing of this book. Roots of Peace is an internationally
renowned humanitarian organization dedicated to eradicating land mines
worldwide and converting war-torn lands into productive farms and wildlife
habitats. Roots of Peace will plant two million fruit and nut trees in Afghanistan
and provide farmers there with the skills and support necessary for sustainable
land use.

Manufactured in China by Insight Editions

10 9 8 7 6 5 4 3 2 1